T0164229

Rescued
from
ISIS Terror

Firas Jumaah
and Charlotta Turner

Rescued from ISIS Terror

How a University Professor Organized
a Commando Mission to Rescue
Her Doctoral Student from Isis-Controlled Iraq

GAUDIUM

Gaudium Publishing
Las Vegas ◊ Oxford ◊ Palm Beach

Published in the United States of America by
Histria Books, a division of Histria LLC
7181 N. Hualapai Way, Ste. 130-86
Las Vegas, NV 89166 USA
HistriaBooks.com

Gaudium Publishing is an imprint of Histria Books. Titles published under the imprints of Histria Books are distributed.

All rights reserved. No part of this book may be reprinted or reproduced or utilized in any form or by any electronic, mechanical or other means, now known or hereafter invented, including photocopying and recording, or in any information storage or retrieval system, without the permission in writing from the Publisher.

Library of Congress Control Number: 2020944038

ISBN 978-1-59211-061-2 (hardcover)
ISBN 978-1-59211-119-0 (softbound)

Copyright © 2021 by Histria Books

Table of Contents

Preface

Throughout history, the Yazidi people have suffered many attempts at genocide at the hands of Islamic militants. Stories told by Yazidi grandparents to their grandchildren or chronicled in poems and folk songs, preserve a record of these attempts at extermination. Because of a dearth of historical documentation, the details of many of these massacres have been lost.

I remember well when my father would sit listening to Kurdish songs, sung by men from Sinjar. Although I didn't understand the Kurdish language, I could feel the sadness in their melodies. One day, when I saw the pangs of sadness in my father's face, I asked him about the meaning of these songs. He explained to me that they were old ballads that told of the massacres of the Yazidis from long ago.

Islamic militants have waged 73 genocidal campaigns against Yazidis throughout history. Most of these heinous massacres took place at the orders of the sultans of the Ottoman Empire. This much has been documented. I never imagined that I would live to see with my own eyes the 74th attempt at extermination. I do not know if this last one was crueler or more heinous than its predecessors. Still, I know that the crimes committed in this genocide included some of the most abominable acts of savagery that I have ever witnessed, heard, or read about.

This book is based on my personal experience in these events. It documents a part of crimes against humanity committed by the terrorists of the Islamic State against the Yazidi people in August 2014. It also highlights the unique heroism of an angel from Sweden, named Charlotta Turner, whose actions saved the lives of myself and my family during these horrific events. She has kindly consented to join me in telling our story.

Firas Jumaah
Lund, Sweden, 2020

Chapter One

Firas's Story

Black Sunday: Massacre at Mosul
Mosul, Iraq, 22 April 2007

It was six o'clock in the morning when I suddenly heard the rush of footsteps and noise coming from the courtyard of our house. I quickly got out of bed and hurried out of my room to find our neighbor, Mumtaz, standing at the doorway to my father's room. I was terrified and asked myself, "What's Mumtaz doing in our house at this early hour?" The front door stood wide open and Yusuf's dump truck was parked directly in front of the house. I ran to my father's room to find someone lying on his back, covered by a blanket, with two women on either side. My vision was not very clear at this time of morning; the sun was only peeking out above the horizon and the lights were off. The first thing I thought was that the person lying on the floor was my father and that he had died. But when I looked over to the right side of the room, I saw my father sitting on his bed. On the opposite sofa was another neighbor, Kamal, whose house was attached to our own. I remained in shock and kept looking left and right, trying to understand what was happening until I heard my mother, who realized what I was thinking, "Don't panic, my son! It's Barakat."

I looked again at the man stretched out on his back and recognized our neighbor, Barakat, and his mother, Merami, who was sitting on his right side. She was crying and holding her son's hand. My mother sat to his left. As the shock wore off, I greeted everyone, and I was relieved that my father was alright. I went over and sat next to Kamal and asked, "What happened? Why are you sitting in the dark? Why don't you turn on the light?"

"As Yusuf was driving in front of your house, Barakat, who was sitting in the back of the dump truck, fell down on his back," Kamal explained. Then my mother added, "While I was washing my face, I heard a loud noise and then the power went out. I rushed to open the door and saw Barakat lying on his back and writhing in pain. Yusuf and I carried him into the house."

Each morning at this hour, everyone gets up to go to work. Barakat was working with Yusuf in construction, and Yusuf parked his truck, loaded with tools and equipment, such as ladders and barrels, close to his house so they would not be stolen. Every morning, Barakat climbed on the back of the dump truck carrying a wooden stick to move the electricity cables that extended from the columns to the houses.

But on this morning, the electricity cable attached to our house got caught on one of the ladders and broke. It struck the dump truck, causing an electrical shock that stunned Barakat, who fell on his back.

My mother, Mumtaz, and Kamal all worked at the textile factory in Mosul. They used to take the same bus every morning from Bashiqa and Bahzani to the factory in Mosul and then back again in the evening.

"We have to hurry, or we'll miss the bus," Mumtaz said to my mother and Kamal.

Kamal got up quickly, but my mother looked at Barakat and his grieving mother and then she decided not to go to work at the factory.

"I'll stay with Barakat because he needs help. Can you ask for a leave of absence for me for today?" my mother asked. They both agreed and left for work.

Yusuf also went to work. Everyone thought Barakat's injury was minor and that the pain would subside in a short time. My mother asked me to call a taxi to take Barakat to the Shaikhan Hospital, which was located 45 km to the north of Mosul. His mother, Merami, was an old woman, unable to look after her son. His older brother was not at home at the time, so my mother volunteered to take care of Barakat and bring him to the hospital.

The taxi arrived and my mother and I put Barakat in it, then we all left for the Shaikhan Hospital. We arrived at the hospital and waited for over five hours while they conducted numerous tests. He was found to have a fracture in one of his lower back vertebrae.

In the meantime, I phoned my fiancée, Rawya, and apologized for not coming. We were supposed to go together to Mosul at 10:00 am for shopping and complete the preparations for our wedding, less than ten days away. She was a little upset at first, but she understood the situation. Barakat's brother arrived at about 1:00 pm and remained with his brother, so my mother and I returned to Bashiqa.

***

3:00 pm, the same day.

While my friends Naseem, Abdulghani, and six others were returning in a minibus from Mosul University to Bashiqa, two cars intercepted them and forced them to pull over on the side of the road. Naseem and Abdulghani both held master's degrees and worked as lecturers at Mosul University. Both were Yazidis and close friends of mine. The other commuters were also from Bashiqa and Behzani.

Two armed men with masks stepped out of one of the cars and headed toward the minibus, aiming their weapons at the commuters and asking them to show their identification cards.

Several days before, there were warnings that extremist terrorist groups had threatened Yazidis with murder, warning Yazidi inhabitants in a statement that they should leave Mosul immediately because the land on which they lived is Islamic land. But these warnings had not been taken seriously by many Yazidis, who considered them as empty threats, aimed at preventing Yazidis from working in Mosul or intimidating those living in Mosul to leave.

Everyone produced their ID cards, but only Naseem and Abdulghani gave their Mosul University work cards. The two gunmen checked the cards and returned them to their owners one by one, except for Naseem and Abdulghani's cards. The other commuters were all Christians or Muslims.

"Where's your ID card?" The armed man looked at them angrily. The religion of a person is usually written on the ID card, so they had asked for the ID cards to see whether or not they were Yazidi.

"I forgot mine at home." Naseem replied as he tried to hide his fear.

"And you?"

"I lost my ID card and I haven't had the time to get a new one," Abdulghani said, seemingly calm although his heart trembled with fear.

Both took the recent threats seriously and decided not to carry their ID cards with them in anticipation of being caught in an ambush or at a fake checkpoint controlled by extremist groups.

"What's your religion?"

"I'm Muslim." Both answered at the same time.

The masked man looked at both with doubt and suspicion and then went to ask the person who was sitting to the right of Abdulghani:

"Do you know them?"

"Yes!"

"Are they true Muslims?"

He paused before answering and then looked at both Naseem and Abdulghani.

"Why don't you answer? Tell me the truth or I'll kill you!" The gunman shouted loudly.

He trembled with fear, for he didn't know what to say. If he told the truth, both his colleagues would be killed, and if he lied, maybe he would be killed. Just before he gave his answer, the gunman's phone rang. There was a state of silence. Everyone looked at the gunman, who was apparently receiving instructions from someone. He hung up the phone and then turned to the other terrorist and said: "We have to go right now because we have an urgent task."

The two gunmen left quickly for an unknown destination. Naseem, Abdulghani and the other passengers were in shock.

"What are you waiting for?" one passenger yelled at the driver, who sat frozen in his seat.

"Go as fast as you can and don't stop, no matter what happens," another said.

The driver recovered himself and quickly made his way to Bashiqa.

***

5:00 pm, the same day.

I was sitting with Rawya in her house, which was nearby. We were neighbors and lived on the same street. I apologized to her for being unable to go to Mosul because of what happened to Barakat and then we started planning for our wedding day. In the meantime, my phone rang. It was my friend, Waad, a policeman in the Mosul city hall.

"Hello, Waad."

"Hello, Firas. where are you?"

"I'm sitting with my fiancée in her house."

"I need to see you right away!"

From the tone of his voice, I knew there was something wrong.

"What's going on?"

"I'll tell you when I see you. I'm close by, on my way to your house. Meet me outside!" Waad said and then hung up the phone.

I was now very worried and I got up to leave.

"What's the matter?!" Rawya asked.

"I don't know, but Waad wants to see me right away for some reason. I'm going to go meet him."

"He may be playing a joke on you. He always calls you when he knows you're with me. I don't know why he doesn't find a girlfriend."

"No! He seemed very serious. I have to go now."

"Don't forget our date tomorrow at 10:00 am to go to Mosul and buy the rest of the wedding supplies. There's not much time left."

"Don't worry, my dear!"

***

A few minutes later.

"Did your mother go to work today?" Waad asked anxiously.

"No, she didn't! Why are you asking about my mother? I questioned him, with surprise and concern.

"That's good news, but I have very bad news."

"What is it? Oh Waad! You're making me very worried."

"I received a call from a colleague who also works as a policeman in the Mosul City Hall. He told me that the bus carrying textile factory workers had been kidnapped by extremist groups and taken to an unknown area. They were all workers from Bashiqa and Bahzani."

"What do you mean?"

"The investigation is still going on. I've asked him to provide me with all of the details."

I remembered that I had Kamal and Mumtaz's phone numbers. I tried to call them, but their phones were off.

"None of the workers are answering their phones. The news has spread throughout the city and everyone is in a state of shock and panic," Waad said.

While we were standing in our alley, people kept coming to the house of our neighbors, Kamal and Mumtaz. Sounds of weeping and wailing of women began to rise from the houses. So far, no one knew if the workers were still alive or had been killed. Waad's phone rang again and he quickly answered. He listened very carefully and only a few seconds later began to show signs of sadness on his face. He hung up the phone and then I asked him eagerly what had happened, but he could not control himself and hugged me as he broke down in tears.

***

Earlier at 3:30pm, that same day.

The workers at the factory had finished for the day and they now boarded the bus to return to their homes in Bashiqa and Bahzani. There were about 35 workers on the bus as it left the factory, 26 of them were Yazidis, the rest were Muslims and Christians. Unusually, the atmosphere of the bus was calm. Everyone was almost silent, with only a few side-conversations going on in low voices. The workers were all from the same city and knew each other well, with close social and family relationships. They would play funny little pranks on each other and share their candy and fruit during the one-hour journey from the textile factory in Mosul to the city of Bashiqa. Among the workers were brothers, fathers, sons, and cousins. Laween sat next to his father, Barakat, and his uncle, Barakat's brother, Khidr, sat behind him. On the bus were also their cousins, Khalil and Omar, all of them from a family called Shabi. Laween was loved by everyone because he was the youngest worker, 21 years old, while the rest of the workers were between 45 and 60 years old. He was a very shy young man who avoided others and talked little, which is why he always stayed close to his father, who in turn took great care of his son. He always sat beside him and defended him, even when the others tried to play tricks on Laween. And because he was single, everyone would joke and ask him if he had an intimate girlfriend or what he would do on his wedding night. Laween's face would turn red as he stuck close to his father even more tightly, then his father would raise his hand, with smile on his face, asking them to stop harassing his son.

"Why is everyone calm today?" Zidu asked, sitting next to Kamal.

"I don't know! But I have a strange feeling and a deep sense of anxiety," Kamal replied.

"And why are you worried?"

"Recently, the threats from the terrorist groups have increased, making our work in Mosul more dangerous."

"Yeah. I hope they are only threats. Our work in the textile factory is the only source of income we have to provide for our families." Zidu kept silent for a moment and then added, "Don't worry! Things will be fine."

"I hope so," Kamal replied. Then they both kept silent.

What was up with this silence? With the quiet uneasiness? Was it the calm before the storm? Or was it the noise of the soul that diminishes when death nears, to make it easier for death to seize the soul from the body. The workers had no idea that the vehicles of death were following behind them.

A few minutes later, armed vehicles intercepted the bus and forced it to pull over. A number of masked gunmen stormed the bus, made their weapons visible to the workers, and ordered the workers to remain silent and not to move or use their mobile phones, or else they would be killed. The workers followed the terrorist's orders. The gunmen collected their phones and turned them off, while another gunman ordered the bus driver to drive to the Al-Nour neighborhood, a densely populated area of Mosul.

Everyone was terrified, but Laween, the youngest, was most afraid. He held on tightly to his father's arm. His father, also frightened, held his son Laween's hand as if he feared they would take him away. The bus stopped in the Al-Noor neighborhood and the gunmen ordered the workers to get off the bus. The gunmen checked the ID cards of each worker and separated out the Yazidi workers, while ordering the non-Yazidi workers to leave. The factory workers were divided into two groups. The first group included nine workers, while the second group included seventeen. Laween, his father, and his uncle were in the second group. Each group was then taken to an empty spot — undeveloped land, situated within the heavily populated area where the terrorists ordered them to lay flat on their stomachs in front of a wall. People had gathered around to witness the executions.

Kamel, Mumtaz, Zidou, and the rest of the Yazidi factory workers got down on their stomachs and then the gunmen opened automatic fire on them. Laween cried out in terror and put his hands over his ears, while his father, who lay next to him, tried to cover him with his own body to save his son's life, but the bullets ripped through the father's body and tore through his son's as well.

Gunmen rotated heavily to make certain that no worker was left alive. After carrying out their horrific crime, the terrorists left, shouting, "Allahu Akbar!... Allahu Akbar!" leaving behind them the bodies of innocent factory workers who had been riddled with bullets.

Only two workers survived the massacre. One of them, Baseem Rashid Jumaah, who was in the first group, miraculously survived after being struck by three bullets, but he lost his brother, Jumaah Rashid Jumaah, in this slaughter. The second survivor was Zidu, who was in the second group. He survived because he ended up on the left side of the "wall of execution," and the murderer's ammunition had run out just as they approached him to finish their heinous deed. But he had still been struck by four bullets; one in the left hand, another in his right hand, a third bullet breaking the bone of his left thigh, and the fourth piercing his chest.

Zidu tried to raise his head slightly to make sure the terrorists were gone. He looked to his right to see the bodies of his co-workers, then he painstakingly looked around to see the people who had stood by to witness the execution beginning to leave without offering any help. He turned to his left and saw houses nearby. He gathered all his strength and began to crawl toward them in search of help, but most of them refused to offer any assistance and prevented him from entering their homes, closing their doors in his face. He tried to crawl from house to house, and blood flowed from him so profusely that he almost lost consciousness. Then someone finally took pity on him when they saw his condition and called for an ambulance.

***

The day after the massacre, we all stood in our alleyway, young and old, men and women, friends, relatives, and neighbors, expecting the arrival of the bodies of Mumtaz and Kamal. This scene was repeated in many of the alleys and streets of Bashiqa and Bahzani. Finally, the first body arrived, which had been placed in a wooden box, wrapped in Kurdistan flag and loaded on the back of a pick-up truck. The sounds of crying rose throughout both towns. The women began to wail and slap their faces and pull their hair, while some of them passed-out from intense grief. We did not know whose body it is was. Was it Kamal or Mumtaz? We ran behind the car, which narrowly made its way through the crowd of people and stopped in front of Kamal's house. We carried the wooden coffin and brought it into the house and placed it in one of the rooms. We took Kamal's body out of the coffin. This was the first time I saw a dead body.

Kamal did not die immediately. He was found alive among the bodies at the scene and was taken to the hospital for treatment, but he died later in the hospital. I removed the gauze and bandages from his stomach and chest. All the injuries were to his chest and abdomen. We washed his legs and hands with warm water and then wrapped him in a shroud, then we placed him in a wooden box, wrapped it in Kurdistan flag and carried him to the cemetery which would be his last resting place. I learned later that Mumtaz's body had been torn apart by the bullets, making it difficult to identify him.

After we completed the burial ceremonies, I returned to our alley with my friend Waad. When we passed by my fiancé's house, I heard her calling me. She was waiting for me on the balcony.

"Okay! I will leave you now, see you later," Waad said, and then left off on his own. As for me, I remained standing, waiting for Rawya to come down.

"You are welcome to come in!" Rawya said.

"I am very tired."

"I know that, but please come in for a few minutes. I need to speak with you."

I went inside and sat down, then she brought a glass of water. I had difficulty swallowing the water because of the intense fatigue I felt after all that I had seen that day. I still could not believe that only yesterday I was sitting with Kamal in our house. Today, I washed his body and put a shroud on him and buried him with my own hands. My hand was trembling as I lifted the glass of water to my lips.

"I can't believe what's happening. They killed them all. Why? What's going on?" she said, crying.

"I don't know! The situation has become very dangerous. I'm shocked and I don't understand what is happening either."

"What do we do now? No one can go to work or study in Mosul anymore. How will these people feed their families? Death waits for everyone there. Mosul has become a city of terror and death. Do not tell me you will return to work at the University of Tikrit! I'm afraid for you."

"I cannot think of anything right now. I cannot get the picture of Kamal out of my mind. You and I were about to go to Mosul to buy the rest of things for our wedding party. What if Barakat did not fall in front of our house? If we went to Mosul, maybe they would have arrested us. Oh! And my mother! She was supposed to go to work today. If she had gone, she might be dead too. Mom! I have to go to see her now."

***

When I returned home, it was nearly sunset. I went into the living room and found my mother sitting on a floor mat next to my father, both leaning against the wall. My brothers and sisters sat around them. My mother was crying, and my father's eyes were also filled with tears. The rest of the family was also sad and crying. I went and sat next to my mother. My father lit a cigarette and blew out its smoke as if to signify his heartbreak. I tried to speak, but I was afraid that I would break down and cry. I could no longer hold back my emotions and, moments later, I too began to cry, and I put my hands on my head. My mother turned to hug me, and I put my head on her chest and wept.

Later that night, as I laid in my bed, smoking a cigarette and blowing the smoke away, watching it spread throughout the room, I thought about what happened and I could see the faces of all the victims floating about my room in the smoke. My mother would likely have been among them, and perhaps I would also be dead, had fate not intervened. Was its destiny that Barakat fell in front of our house and prevented us from going to Mosul? Or was there an angel watching over us?

Work at Tikrit University became impossible. Now I had to find another solution. "Maybe I can find a job at a university in the Kurdistan region," I thought to myself.

Chapter Two

Firas's Story

Duhok, Iraq, Three years later, 2010

We had postponed our wedding because of the massacre at Mosul. Several months later, on September 20, 2007, we had a very small wedding ceremony. We invited only a few relatives and close friends, out of respect for the families of the victims in Bashiqa and Bahzani. During this period, I left my job as a lecturer at Tikrit University and managed to find a job as a lecturer at the University of Zakho, which is in the province of Duhok in the Kurdistan region of Iraq. Rawya abandoned her studies at the University of Mosul for security reasons. She then continued her studies to attain her bachelor's degree in chemistry at the Faculty of Science at the University of Duhok. The laboratories at the University of Zakho lacked modern equipment and the teaching still depended on the use of old and traditional methods and devices. However, this was not a big problem compared to what I endured during my studies at Mosul University and my work at Tikrit University.

The biggest problem I faced in Iraq was that of racial discrimination. The cultural heritage shared by the people of Iraq is different based on the region they inhabit, their race, religion, and the community to which they belong. This includes religious heritage, customs, traditions, values, ethical standards, and attitudes toward other peoples. In terms of religious heritage, it includes all that is written and unwritten about ideas, symbols, laws, and values, which have become entrenched into the everyday behavior of individuals. Normally, there shouldn't be an issue with cultural differences between people living in the same country, but problems arise when individuals do not accept the cultural heritage of others.

During my studies and work in Mosul and Tikrit — areas with an Arab majority — I was often, directly, or indirectly, exposed to harassment and racial discrimination based on my ethnicity and religion. I am Kurdish and many Arabs make jokes that ridicule Kurds. They consider Kurds to be less intelligent. Many times, they bragged and shouted out jokes in front of me, without any shame, while others laughed. Some Arabs do not even consider Kurds to be human beings, they say they are from the Djinn. There are many legends concerning the origins of the Kurds. One of these legends had been created in the neighboring societies by the Arabs details the Kurds as being the descendants of King Solomon's angelic servants (Djinn). This legend says that King Solomon, who ruled over the supernatural world, called his angelic servants and ordered them to fly to Europe for the sake of bringing to him 500 beautiful maidens. By the time they were done and the servants returned to Israel, the king had already died. The Djinn settled in the mountains, and they retained those women for themselves, and their offspring formed the Kurdish nation.

I also suffered from religious discrimination because I was a Yazidi living in the midst of a Muslim community. Many of them considered me an infidel, so I often avoided revealing my religious identity for fear of being killed. Yazidis are people living mainly in northern Iraq, who speak the Kurdish language and believe in the Yazidi religion. The Yazidis were influenced by some of the region's civilizations, such as the Assyrians, the Babylonians, and some Jewish communities. Elements of the Zoroastrian civilization in Persia were merged with the Yazidis. The Yazidis are the oldest religion in the world, and they emphasize this because of their ancient historical calendar dating back more than 6,700 years. The word 'Yazidis' is derived from the ancient Persian term "yazata," which means the holy, or "Yazdan," which means The God.

The Yazidis believe that God created seven angels of His light led by the Archangel, called the "Melek Taus." The Yazidis reject rumors that they are worshiped by "Satan;" in fact, they do not believe in the existence of an evil being like the "Devil" and consider evil to come from man himself.

The Lalish Temple is the main religious temple of the Yazidis and there is a pilgrimage to it, which is located in the valley of Lalish or "Valley of Silence" in Iraq, as it is a very ancient temple that some historians say dates back to the third century BC. The Yazidis have been subjected to dozens of extermination campaigns, especially by Muslims, who consider them infidels and devil worshipers. Hundreds of thousands of Yazidis have been killed during these genocide campaigns and their civilization is on the verge of extinction. More than 20 million Yazidis were killed during the genocide of the Yazidis during their history. The most recent of these attacks was the Islamic State's attacks on them, killing 4,000 Yazidis, abducting more than 6,500, gang-raping 2,000 of them, and selling over 1,500 as slaves.

The Iraqi people are characterized by the most primitive forms of discrimination — discrimination on the basis of race and religion, which has been rejected by most other cultures and peoples.

When I wanted to get out of the house, I was confused and wondering to myself whether it was more appropriate to carry a civil ID card or leave it at home. That card differentiated between Iraqis on the basis of ethnicity, religion and doctrine. This was not just my feeling, it was the feeling of most Iraqis. Everyone was afraid of being kidnapped or killed because of sectarian violence, or being harassed by security personnel for sectarian reasons.

The anxiety and fear increased after the Mosul massacre because of the spread of armed terrorist groups. It had become difficult to distinguish between a security man and a terrorist. So, I often preferred to sit at home and not go out, except in extreme cases.

The killing in Iraq has become linked to the State IDs which indicate the holder's religious identity. And even if you don't carry your ID with you, your name may be the cause of your death. The extremist terrorist groups can distinguish any religion or sect from a name. For example, if your name is Peter, John, or Micah, you are Christian. If your name is Hamou, Salou, or Kamshou, you are Yazidi, and if your name is Othman, Sufyan, or Omar, you are a Sunni Muslim, and if your name is Karrar, Haider, or Abdulzahra, you are a Shiite Muslim.

Sectarian violence hit Iraq in 2005. Extremist armed groups from both the Shiite and Sunni communities began to set up fake checkpoints and began killing people according to the religion mentioned on their IDs or even by their names. Thousands have been killed as a result of these practices.

***

In 2010, my wife and I lived in a small apartment in Duhok. We had a two-year-old boy named Maxim, and Rawya was pregnant. I was commuting from Duhok to the University of Zakho every day by bus and the journey took about one hour. Rawya was a junior at the University of Duhok.

Abdulghani and Naseem also moved to the University of Zakho. In 2008, Abdulghani got a scholarship from the Erasmus Mundus Program to do doctoral studies at Lund University in Sweden, and a year later, Naseem also got a scholarship from the same program to do his doctoral studies at Lund University.

I also dreamed of getting a Ph.D. scholarship outside of Iraq for several reasons. The first was that all the laboratories in Iraq lacked modern facilities and equipment, and the second, which was the most important for me, was that I wanted to learn about new cultures and experience other societies. I was in constant contact with Abdulghani and Naseem and they provided me with information on the most important programs and the dates of deadlines for the applications, as well as tips on how to apply to increase my chances of getting a scholarship.

One day, Abdulghani called me and told me about a one-year scholarship for partial doctoral program at Lund University in Sweden. Despite being a scholarship for only one year, it was a golden opportunity that I may not have found again. I applied for this grant and fortunately, I received it. I was very happy, but I had to make the decision together with my wife, especially as she was not yet finished with her university studies. We discussed it and decided to go together in the hope that I would receive a full scholarship in the future. Rawya decided to temporarily abandon her studies and travel with me, especially since she was pregnant and I could not leave her alone with Maxim, who was only two years old at the time.

A few months later, we traveled from Bashiqa to Syria to apply for a visa for Sweden, as there was no Swedish Embassy in Iraq. It was necessary for me to enter the European Union before September 1st, otherwise the scholarship would be canceled. We waited for several days for the decision of the Swedish Embassy, but it kept getting delayed. Rawya and I were in a state of anxiety. There were only a few days left, so I called Abdulghani and told him about my situation, then he contacted the immigration office in Sweden to try to speed up the decision.

On August 30, 2010, we finally received the visa and I was able to book a flight for that the same day. At 8:00 pm, our flight took off from Damascus International Airport and entered European Union airspace before 12:00 pm, landing first in Hungary at the airport in Budapest. A few hours later, the connecting flight left for Copenhagen, where we were greeted by Naseem. We took the train to Lund, across the Öresund Bridge, arriving at Lund around 4 pm. We went to Abdulghani's apartment where his wife had prepared lunch for us.

For Rawya and I, everything was new and strange but beautiful and positive. We looked at the faces of the people, their clothes, the signs hanging and written in languages other than Arabic. Even the air was refreshing, cool, and very clean. From time to time, I drew a deep breath and held it in my diaphragm for as long as I could, and then I released it, as if I trying to cleanse my lungs from dust. When we crossed the Öresund Bridge, Maxim looked out over the Baltic Sea through the window with a big smile on his face. We were all very happy, it was the first time we saw a body of water of this size, the first time we rode on a train, and the first time we flew on an airplane. In fact, this was the first time we had ever traveled outside of Iraq.

***

A few days later, I went to the Chemical Center at Lund University and met Christina, the student affairs officer, who guided me to the lecture hall as my course had already started the day before. I entered the classroom and sat down. There was an old man with a dark brown beard named Professor Jan Åke who was explaining one of the slides on his power point presentation. As he talked, one of the students interrupted him "Jan Åke! Jan Åke!" I was surprised at this behavior. How could a student interrupt a professor in this way without raising his hand and asking for permission to speak? And how could he call him by his name without his title? Initially, I thought the professor would be upset by this behavior, but I was surprised by the way he responded. He turned to the student and began to listen attentively to him. Then he answered the question in a way that showed his professionalism and expertise. After making sure that the student understood his answer, he continued his lecture. In my country, a student would not be allowed to call a professor by his name without mentioning his title, and this was true even among colleagues.

I looked around at the students in the lecture hall and I saw that they were mostly from different countries. But what drew my attention was that many of them drank coffee and chewed gum during the lecture. In my country, the students would receive a warning or, in many cases, be expelled from class for such behavior. After completing the lecture, I toured the Chemical Center, which was very large building and included numerous classrooms, as well as laboratories equipped with the latest instruments.

***

On Saturday, October 30, my wife began to experience labor pains. At 11:00 pm, I called the hospital and told them about my wife's condition. They asked me to bring her to the hospital right away. I called a taxi and we went to the hospital together with Maxim. They placed Rawya in a private room and, after doing some tests, the nurse told us that

Rawya might give birth within the next few hours. Maxim slept on the couch in the room. At about 2:00 am on Sunday October 31, it was time for Rawya to give birth. I carried Maxim, who was still asleep, and took him outside of the room and placed him on a chair in the hallway. I went back in the room to be with my wife as she gave birth. About thirty minutes later, she gave birth to a beautiful little girl. We named her Enana, the name of a Sumerian goddess, Ishtar, the god of love, sex, beauty, desire, and fertility. It was very strange for me to have the opportunity to be with my wife as she gave birth. When she gave birth in Iraq to our first child, Maxim, it was forbidden for me to be in the room. This experience was something new and strange, but it was also beautiful.

***

After several months of study, I passed several courses, but I started to worry because my scholarship was nearly halfway over, and I had not yet received a full scholarship. I decided to get a second master's degree in Chemistry during the time I had left on my scholarship.

In April 2011, I joined the Green Technology group, GTG, as a master's degree student under the supervision of Professor Charlotta Turner, Lotta. At the end of October 2011, I managed to get a scholarship from the Kurdistan region in. Iraq.

In December 2011, I went with my family to Iraq to visit my family and to sign the contract for the scholarship that I obtained from the Kurdistan region in Iraq. We also decided to celebrate the new year with our families in Iraq. We all were happy, especially my parents, that I finally managed to get full scholarship for doctoral study at Lund University in Sweden.

On January 8, 2012, when I was returning home at twelve o'clock in the afternoon, after spending quality time with my friends in the cafeteria, I encountered my sister Sondos as she was on her way to our house. My sister is married to my cousin Thamer and she lives in Bashiqa. We hugged and then headed home together. Only my father and my brother's wife, Linda, were in the house. Linda was busy in the kitchen preparing food. My mother was still at work. She now worked at the textile factory in Bartella, 25 kilometers south of Bashiqa. She moved to work in this factory after the massacre of her fellow workers in the Mosul textile factory.

Rawya and the children were at her father's house on this day. Sondos went to my father's room to say hello to my father, while I went to my room to change my clothes. As soon as I entered my room I heard my sister Sondos screaming. I ran to my father's room and found my father lying face-down while Sondos was screaming as she tried hard to turn him on his back. I turned my father on his back. My heart almost leapt from my chest from fear. I grabbed his hand, which was as cold as ice, to feel for his pulse, but I couldn't feel anything. I asked Sondos to call my brother Fares, who works in Bashiqa health center, and to ask him to come with the ambulance. I tried to give my father CPR, but it was too late. My father had passed away from a stroke.

My joy in obtaining the scholarship was short-lived. My father's death shocked me and caused me immense grief. He had wanted this opportunity so badly for me and now he would no longer be there to share in it. It took me a long time to recover from his loss. It was an ominous start to my Ph.D. studies.

Chapter Three

Lotta's Story

From Uppsala to Lund, Sweden, 4th of March 2010

T he long journey on the train from Uppsala to Lund is just what I needed. Peace and quiet. Time to think about everything that is happening in my life right now. The snow covering the ground outside the cold damp train window spread out in the distance. We have just passed Älmhult, a small town that is best known for the place where Ingvar Kamprad grew up during the 20s and 30s, and where he founded Ikea in 1943. Tired, I lean my forehead against the train window. The dense fir forest is buzzing by as I think that I will probably have to spend a lot of time in Ikea in the near future. In a week, the moving truck will go from Uppsala to Lund, then the rest of my family — my husband and two children — will join.

What am I really getting myself into? Was it really the right decision to move to Lund? We are doing so well in Uppsala, and my husband, Kuria, commutes distance in the capital Stockholm for work. Admittedly, Kuria does not have the best prospects as a young researcher at Stockholm University. Since his boss tragically passed away in a malignant cancer, Kuria has not been given the academic freedom he so desperately wanted. The new boss does not understand why it might be interesting to analyze iron and carbon dioxide absorption capacity in seawater in and around Antarctica. I enjoy being a young researcher at Uppsala University, besides the fact that I would love to teach chemistry courses. I love to be in contact with students, teaching chemistry to others, but I don't get that opportunity in Uppsala; there are already too many teaching researchers at the department.

I close my eyes and try to sleep for a while. The train turns in the long curves and I begin to feel slightly nauseous. A child cries further in the back of the carriage. Two older women talk a little too loudly in front of me. Maybe I should have taken a motion sickness tablet after all; high-speed trains often make me nauseous. I get up to go to the bathroom but turn away right in the door as the scent of the urine strikes me. The train suddenly shakes a little extra, then stabilizes in the next second. In the restaurant wagon, I buy a cup of coffee and a cinnamon bun to calm both my nausea and slight hunger. I struggle on my way back to the seat. My thoughts are slipping away, and I am thinking about the interview I will give for TV tomorrow. They want to interview me for the large research grant I have recently received. My research is about extracting valuable molecules from industrial vegetable waste, such as onion peels or waste carrots.

Chemistry, especially analytical chemistry, is my great passion in life. With the large research grant of 2 million EUR, I will be able to do a lot of interesting research. I really want to investigate the new environmentally friendly processes where instead of using toxic chemicals, you only use water or pressurized carbon dioxide that you can be reused in the processes. If it is also possible to use biomass that is usually regarded as waste, then it will be even more environmentally sustainable! I am sure this is what the journalist on TV would like to hear tomorrow, I think confidently.

Apparently, the head of the Department of Chemistry at Lund University also likes my research profile. Or maybe it's just the fact that I just got a big research grant that he likes... and that I now plan to take my ideas with me from Uppsala to Lund. One day a few months ago, the head of department called me and asked if I was interested in an employment opportunity at Lund University. I was hand-picked. Head hunted. It felt really flattering. Now I'm sitting here on a train towards Lund. The adventure has begun.

We roll in towards Lund Central Station and the train stops with an extended squeak and a final judder. It smells of burnt oil. People are crowded in the compartment to take down their damp suitcases from the shelves. A young guy behind me is too close, and I feel his elbow digging into my back as he puts on his scarf. I bend down and look out over the platform outside. It looks grey and cold. Apparently, there is snow in Lund even though we are so far south in

Sweden. It is unusual for the snow to remain so late in the season. I manage to get out of the hot, damp train with my luggage bag in tow. Finally, I am in Lund.

***

5th of March 2010

The interview with the journalist went well. Sometimes I find it difficult to explain my research in a simple and interesting way, so that the public sees the environmental benefits of chemistry. The sun is shining, and it looks like the last of the snow is finally melting away. I walk from Östra Mårtensgatan in Lund, along the eastern part of the Botanical Garden. I make a spontaneous decision and turn right onto Linnégatan. On the corner of Celsiusgatan-Linnégatan, I stop and look at the beautiful gardener's villa in front of me. Linnégatan 7. A rusty-red brick villa on two floors with a tower decorated with a tetrahedron shaped copper roof. On the south side, the vines climb eagerly up the house wall. The house has beautiful windows with wooden carved details, and the large lush garden is filled with fruit trees. This is where I grew up.

I can't help feeling nostalgic as I look at the beautiful house in front of me. I lived here during the early 1970s, when I was a little girl. I have many memories of playing around with my little sister, Pernilla, and the dog, Bamse, who was a big black furry Bouvier des Flandres. Sometimes

I climbed up on the high copper roof with my father, Bengt, and there we sat together and looked out over the rooftops in Professor's Town in Lund. You might think that I grew up in an upper-class family in Lund, but it wasn't that simple. My father, on the other hand, grew up in a right-wing home in Borås, and it was partly thanks to his father that my parents were able to buy the beautiful villa in Lund. To afford all the expenses, my parents rented the entire upstairs of the house to students who needed a home in Lund. We had an American couple, a young man from China, and two students from Sweden living in the house. I remember evenings when one of the students picked up his guitar and played left-wing songs about the war in Vietnam. We sat on the floor and ate rice with chopsticks, and the adults talked about freedom, women's struggle and the labor movement. I think I was formed during my first years in Lund. From my parents, I learned about people's equal value, and about opening your home to those in need. I learned to listen to those who speak. In my childhood, I heard stories from all corners of the world.

I look in through the gate to the garden and see that it is just as beautiful as I remember it. However, it looks a little smaller. Suddenly, my chest tightens as I think of my father, Bengt, and how we used to do carpentry together in the basement of the house. Butter knives, cutting boards and fantasy figures. Almost exactly three years ago, my father passed away in malignant cancer; T-cell lymphoma. It went so fast, far too fast. My older son, Elias, was only four years old, and my younger son was not even born. In fact, my husband and I tried for several years to get pregnant again. We so wanted our son to have a sibling. During my father's funeral in April 2007, I received a small guardian angel in gilded brass. Then, as a little angel, our second son was born in December of that year. His name is Gabriel.

I take a deep breath and look through the windows of the villa one last time before walking further along Linnégatan. Lund is a beautiful little town. With about 90,000 inhabitants, half of whom are students, it gives a young and energetic impression. It feels exciting to move back here after living in both California and Uppsala for several years. I wonder how my two sons will like it here. My husband, Kuria, who is originally from Kenya, knows Lund well because of his time as a doctoral student here. We met in Lund in the 90's when we were both PhD students in analytical chemistry. I fell in love with him pretty soon after we met. A kinder and more patient person cannot be found. One of the things I like about my husband is how generously and empathetically he looks at people from different countries and cultures. Although we have such an incredibly different upbringing, my husband in rural Kenya and I on Linnégatan in Lund, we have very similar values.

I quickly walk up Tornavägen to stay warm. The road is lined with large villas, an elementary school with a beautiful park next to it, and a cycle path where masses of students pedal uphill to the university's various departments and lecture halls. There is a hope in the air that spring is on its way. I'm almost hit by a cyclist as I cross the road. Students sometimes bike like crazy; rarely do I see young people wearing bicycle helmets. They risk their lives every day in their bikes. I stop for red light at the junction Tornavägen-Tunavägen. My fingers are frozen, despite the fact that the temperature was above freezing. Thoughts wander away. Will my sons be happy in Lund? Will we find a good school for them? Where should we live? *It will work out*, I tell myself when the light finally turns green and I cross Tunavägen.

I step into the Chemistry Center a few minutes later. It is a giant F-shaped red brick building, totaling 40,000 square meters, that had been built in the 60's. It may sound strange, but I actually think the building is beautiful. I like red bricks. Inside the department I meet my new colleague, Maggan. She and I will jointly lead the research group that I have moved with me from Uppsala.

"Maggan, shall we have a cup of coffee?" I wonder.

"Absolutely," replies Maggan

We sit down in the coffee room and start talking about a course that I will teach. I am so pleased that I finally not only get to be a researcher but also a teacher. The coffee room is large and airy, and along the western part of the coffee room runs a long balcony. I imagine that it will be nice to drink coffee there when it is warmer outside. A number of

sun-worn plastic chairs are lined up along the balcony rail-
ing, and a few are overturned next to them. I do not see if
there are any associated tables. My gaze wanders back into
the room, where I see more and more people entering. It is a
quarter past ten, which is the classic time for morning coffee
in Sweden. It smells of freshly brewed coffee. Younger employees and students hang their lab coats outside the coffee
room. One of the people who step into the room is a man
who seems to be about the same age as myself.

"Hello. I am Ola. I am the manager of this department,"
he tells me.

"Hi, Ola. Charlotta Turner. Or Lotta, as most people call
me," I say.

"Welcome to the chemistry in Lund. I hope you enjoy
it!" says Ola happily.

"Thank you," I say and smile back.

There seems to be a nice and unusually relaxed manager
at this place. Ola is wearing jeans and a worn out T-shirt. I
have never seen a professor with such a washed-out T-shirt
before. He is also wearing crocs slippers. I immediately feel
a great deal of confidence in Ola, but I can't really explain
why. He seems honest and sincere, with his clear, sharp
eyes, and his cunning smile. Ola sits down with a cup of coffee next to me and Maggan.

"When does your family move to Lund?" Maggan asks,
facing me.

"They will come next weekend," I say. "Then the Easter holiday starts and we have time to look at a few different schools and preschools for the children. We also thought of looking at some houses; we do not want to live in the university's loan apartment for too long."

"Tell me if you need help with anything," says Maggan.

I have known Maggan since we were both doctoral students in Lund. She is a warm person who is impossible to dislike. Reliable, helpful and with a big heart. Maggan always thinks the best of people. She was born in Sweden, but her parents are from Greece and moved to Sweden just a couple of years before Maggan was born. Her hair is long and dark, and she has warm dark eyes. Above all, she has one of the sharpest brains I know. It is always inspiring to discuss chemistry with her.

Now, the decision to move to Lund is starting to feel right. In addition, the head of department has promised that I will have several labs for my research group. In Uppsala, I only had a small lab that I shared with some other researchers. The head of department has also promised that I will be able to hire a new doctoral student for my group at the department's expense. I feel selected and special. Finally, my research is truly getting started.

We leave the coffee room after a little chat with my new colleagues. Maggan shows me around the lab in the various premises and also in the course lab. A course in analytical chemistry is in full swing. In front of an analysis instrument in the lab stands a small group of students. I walk up to them and ask what they are doing.

"We analyze antibiotics, Sarafloxacin, in a water sample," says one of the students; a young woman who seemed to be about 20 to 25 years old.

"What is the analysis instrument you use?" I ask.

"A mass spectrometer," says the same student. She looks a little tense at me, like she's wondering why I am questioning her. It's crowded in the lab with about 40 students. The room has large windows, so it's bright and clear with sunlight. On top of benches in long rows are several similar analysis instruments. Along the walls there are more benches with instruments and some ventilated cabinets.

Maggan and I move on through the course lab and into a lab that completely lacks students. It also looks desolately empty on the various benches.

"Here is the lab where we can put the instruments you bring with you from Uppsala. When are they coming?" Maggan asks.

"Everything comes in a truck next week. I do not know exactly which day," I reply.

The benches are reasonably fresh with a few exceptions. Maggan sees me looking at some of the worn tables and says, "We can replace the benches that are not so nice. And this is where we store chemicals."

Inside the lab, she shows various stores and cabinets, tools, instruments and gas bottles. After a while I feel tired of all the walking around in the lab and I suggest we take a lunch together to continue planning.

"Who from your group in Uppsala will move here to Lund?" Maggan asks

"Several actually, which surprises me. I thought that most of them would not be able to move," I say.

"Sofia and Jiayin are doctoral students who have so much time left of their doctoral studies that they wanted to move along to Lund. Several of my postdoctoral fellows will also come to Lund," I tell Maggan.

"It is good that so many people will be moving to Lund. They can also help to get all the instruments in the lab ready," reasoned Maggan

"Yes, absolutely. In addition, the head of department has promised to pay a three-month extension of both Sofia's and Jiayin's doctoral positions so that they are not slowed down too much by the move," I say.

During lunch, we continue to discuss arrangements for routines with meetings, seminars, activities with the group to explain how everything works in Lund in comparison with Uppsala. We sit in the lunch restaurant inside the Ingvar Kamprad Design Center, which was really built after a large donation by Ingvar Kamprad. It is an exciting building, with large space, glass walls and wooden details. The noise level is high, and it is crowded between the dining tables. Chairs stand back to back. The food is good, especially the soup and the vegetarian buffet. It is clear that the restaurant is popular among both students and teachers at the university. Everyone sits mixed here and there, and most are involved in both eating and talking at the same time. The front of the building has an outdoor patio with a coffee table, which will surely be used extensively when the sun is warming.

"Are you ready?" I wonder

"Yes, we can go back to the Chemistry Center," says Maggan

We leave the IKDC, which everyone calls 'the building', cross Sölvegatan and enter through entrance A at the Chemical Center. It is a short walk of 200 meters, but it's still nice to get some fresh air before we continue our discussions indoors. We walk through the long corridor with lab on one side and workspace on the other. I have been given an office at the end of one corridor — a corner room with a nice view of the Astronomy Department's observatory. It is a tower-like building with a telescope on the top floor. I stand in front of my new desk and look out over a parking lot and the observatory further afield. I think that I will really enjoy working here.

***

15th of November 2010

Time has passed so fast. Spring, summer, and autumn. My husband Kuria and our two sons are based in Lund now. Kuria commutes to Stockholm every week, and the children go to school and preschool near our new townhouse. We have a new family member, the rabbit Stampe. He is silky grey with long ears. Stampe lives outdoors in the garden in a small wooden two-story house with a large fence. Stampe's special skill is that he can comfort children who are sad. My mother, Ann-Marie, and father-in-law, Sven Olof, often come to visit, and they help with the kids and the rabbit when I'm on conference trips. In the garden, there is a terrace that we have used several times already for barbecue evenings, sometimes also inviting my research group. Maggan and I lead the group together, and have great joy as we see the younger students and doctoral students develop to become excellent researchers. Maybe we have some future research leaders in our group.

I bike quickly from home to work inside the Chemistry Center. It is grey and drizzling, and I am uncertain whether the sun has yet risen or not. Despite the chilly weather, I feel warm and humid when I arrive at the parking place for bikes outside entrance A to the Chemical Center. I park and lock my bike, my true follower from Uppsala that has a red colored saddle with white spots. I meet a colleague in the corridor to say hello. This colleague, on the other hand, barely greets me. It is clear that winter is coming, and people are low and not quite as happy. I still feel good. It is Monday morning and I will be teaching a course on how to analyze metals in water. This class consists of students in their second and third year of chemistry studies, and it is always inspiring to talk to students.

I hurry into the lecture hall and start my presentation. For once, the technology does not mess with me, and my computer cooperates nicely with the projectors on the ceiling that illuminate the two large screens in the lecture hall. Several students are curious and ask many questions. Others mostly want to know what is important to be able to pass the exam. A few at the back of the hall are half asleep. I don't blame them; it is a quarter past eight on this grey Monday morning.

"Here you see that we can use either an oven, flame or a plasma when analyzing atoms," I say loudly and clearly in the hall. I draw schematic pictures on the chalkboard, and I think that this is extremely interesting information.

"For atomic emission spectroscopy, you can use a CCD detector, just as those you have in cameras. Does anyone know how a CCD works?" I ask right out in the lecture hall.

After a while that feels like an eternity, a student in the front row raises his hand and says, "It's a detector that has many pixels, or ...?"

"Well that's right," I say, relieved that someone answered the question at all. Then I explain in detail the structure of a so-called charged coupled device.

After the lecture, I feel both tired and satisfied. I think it went well. The students did not ask any questions that I could not answer. This is just my second semester as a teacher at Lund University, and I still feel unsure about the pedagogics. I go straight to the coffee room, because now I need a cup of strong coffee with milk. I take a mug in the cupboard above the sink, and head off to the automatic coffee machine which is just inside the door to the balcony. It is my boss Ola who stands before me in the queue for the desirable drink. It takes an eternity to make each cup of coffee, for the beans first need to be ground in the machine before rolling down to the coffee filter.

"All is well?" Ola asks

"Yes, absolutely," I answer. "I've been teaching."

"What course is it?" Ola wonders.

"KEMB06, the basic course in analytical chemistry," I say. "It went fine."

After some polite talk and Ola's joke about the new vice chancellor who became a professor almost entirely without any academic merits and who is also so religious, it's finally my turn to get coffee. I push the plastic button that starts the process of grinding beans and brewing coffee. The machine grunts and after a few minutes the caffeine-rich black drink runs down my mug.

I bring my coffee mug into my office. It's not like I don't have the time to sit down in the coffee room to be social with my colleagues. Quite often, I actually prefer to sit for myself in front of the computer and work on writing an article or responding to emails. As I am deeply immersed in reading a manuscript from one of my doctoral students, someone gently knocks on the door. I look up and see that it is Firas, the student from Iraq who is now working on his master degree. Firas is one of the more mature master students, perhaps five or ten years older than the others. He has dark hair, a high hairline, and his eyes are quite small, round, and give a friendly impression. My office door is closed but it has a large glass window. I wave my hand eagerly as a sign that he can come in.

"Hi, Firas," I say.

"Hello," replies Firas. "Is it OK for me to come in?"

"Of course, come in," I say, shifting my focus from my computer to Firas. "What's on your mind?"

"Something happened in the lab," Firas says, looking a little ashamed. "I opened the pressurized sample container carelessly, and the sample sprayed up into the ceiling. Unfortunately, there are bilberry spots in the roof now."

It goes quiet for a few seconds. Then I can't keep myself from laughing. I burst out in a loud laugh and Firas begins to smile gently. Did he think I would get angry at him? Geez, anyone can make mistakes, and that was a fun mistake! I am immediately interested in hearing how this went, and how much bilberry extract is now in the ceiling. When I recover after the laughter, I ask Firas, "How did this really happen? How are things going with your degree project?"

"I have no new results, but this one with the leak, or whatever you want to call it... the whole ceiling has blue dots now..." Firas says, still with a shameful expression in his eyes.

"Let's go down together to the laboratory and look at your artwork," I say grinning.

I'm not really annoyed. On the contrary, I think it's important to point out that everyone can make mistakes. The worst thing that can happen is if students or doctoral students do not dare to talk about their mistakes, and instead pretend that everything is going well, even if it is not. It can then take a very long time for a project to progress. Or at least, it is more difficult to build trust between supervisor and student if there are untold aspects or even lies.

Once down in the research laboratory, we stare up at the ceiling above the extraction equipment used by Firas. I am admiring the blue-colored art, and he looks somewhat distressed.

"Yes, it will not be so easy to wash the ceiling," I explain. "This will be a memory of your degree projects," I say as I continue giggling.

"OK, I guess so," Firas says, shaking his head lightly.

"But how is the project going, aside from the blueberries being sprayed on the ceiling?" I wonder.

"It's not going well," says Firas. "Using pressurized carbon dioxide as an extractant does not work well for the pigments in the blueberries. Instead, it seems that I extract oil from the berries," Firas mentions, a little doubtful.

"OK, but that's exciting! We could change the direction of your project and instead of pigment extract the oil from the bilberry," I say with new energy. "Can you check if anyone has investigated this before? Search in the literature for blueberries, lipids, and extraction," I instruct.

"OK, I'll do that," Firas replies.

I leave the lab thinking that this degree project isn't going well, but Firas is really determined. He is a mature student, and he has ambition. In addition, he has strong social skills and all people in the group like him. In the end, the bilberry study will be a fine work, which may even be the basis of a scientific article. Well, unless he continues to spray paint walls and ceilings in the lab, I think as I grin and go into my office to continue the work of revising a manuscript.

***

Maputo, Mozambique, 6th of July 2012

I wake up with a twitch as the airplane bounces against the ground, rapidly slowing down on the runway off Maputo in Mozambique. The journey here was long, but I got a lot of work done on the plane. My presentation for the conference is ready; I've fine-tuned it almost to perfection. I will present research results from all the doctoral students in my group, including results from Firas. Now he is accepted as a doctoral student in my group, thanks to a scholarship from the human capacity development program of the Kurdistan Region of his home country, Iraq. There will be a scientific article on extraction of bilberry oil, but it is far from finished. There are still a lot of experiments for Firas to complete before his work is finished.

I am also wondering if I should photograph the beach in Maputo and insert it as a closing picture in my presentation. It feels polite to show appreciation to the researchers who actually live here in Maputo, and who have invited me to this conference.

"The chemists have landed," I say in a rough drowsy voice to Amira, who is sitting next to me. Amira is a postdoctoral fellow in my group, and she will also present her research at the conference on analytical chemistry.

"Yes, it's nice to finally arrive," Amira replies.

She smiles at me and looks completely rested and is as beautiful as usual. She is from Sudan, and she has big dark eyes and a fairly dark skin. I don't know what her hair looks like because it's loosely covered with an Islamic veil. Only a few millimeters of her hair can be seen in the hairline above her forehead. I imagine her hair is certainly as beautiful as her face. Amira moved with me from Uppsala to Lund, and she is a calm and pleasant person to be associated with. She is educated in food chemistry, and in my group, she has developed several new analytical methods for plants and foods of various kinds.

However, Amira's family situation is much more complicated than her research. She is engaged to a man from Eritrea who is living in California. This man has not been approved of by her father. Amira has been repeatedly threatened by his father and brother. Her mother was very supportive of her, yet helpless in front of her husband, Amira's father. The family lives in Sudan, but is occasionally in Sweden. However, since the outbreak of the conflict around Amira's fiancé, she never knows when the family is around, and she is always worried that the father or her brother will seek her out to harm her, or try to force her back to Sudan. Amira's dream is to have an academic career, not to marry a man in Sudan whom her parents choose for her to marry. In Lund, I saw no other way out than to make sure that her accommodation and phone number was kept a secret to protect her. I admire Amira for her determination and stubbornness; I know from my own experience that with a thick forehead, you can go a long way.

Amira and I hustle ourselves out of the airplane, pick up our suitcases and get a ride with the conference organizers to the hotel. We will be staying at the Southern Sun Hotel, which is located on the extremely beautiful beach in Maputo. There will be great opportunities to see beautiful sunrises here, I think as I look out over the beach. Maybe you can also run along the beach, if there is some time for it during the conference.

***

The next morning, we have a fantastic breakfast in the hotel dining room. A chef with a tall white hat prepares an omelet for me with all the ingredients I want, and I eat until I am stuffed. The coffee is also good, which is not always something you can count on when you are traveling. Amira and I catch a conference bus to the congress building and take one of the front rows of the lecture hall. An eternally long opening ceremony is taking place, where all sorts of important people welcome us. Ministers, the city mayor, a vice chancellor, the conference chair, among others. There will also be some musical entertainment on stage. After an hour or two, we are finally released from the room to spread out in different parallel sessions.

Before the actual scientific conference starts, we have a coffee break with a lot of delicious snacks. I stand at a round high table dressed with fancy white cloth and talk to Amira and another of the conference attendees. We are in a good mood, joking about one thing and the other. Suddenly I see two men making their way among coffee-drinking conference attendees. They have their eyes fixed only on Amira, and they do not look friendly when they walk toward us with determined steps. On the contrary, they appear to be extremely annoyed. I don't understand why. There is not a nicer person than Amira. You can hardly be in a conflict with her, I think, when they all of a sudden start to attack her verbally. I see the fear in Amira's eyes. The tension between the two men and Amira is vibrating in the air.

"Are you from Sudan?" one of the men asks in Arabic.

The man, who has a name tag from the conference just like us, appears to be in his 60s. He has a dark grey suit and is almost completely bald. His dark grey hair is like a wreath around his head. The other man is in his 40s and is also dressed in suit, but has significantly more hair on his head.

"Yes," Amira answers doubtfully in Arabic to the older man.

She looks at me, and I see her insecurity expressed in her face. The man replicates like a shotgun, still in Arabic, "Where in Sudan are you from? Which city? What's your father's name? What are you doing here? Are you married? Is your husband with you here?"

The atmosphere is now even more threatening. I feel stiff, and I can't think of what to say. I think I should tell the man to leave us alone, but I can't bring myself to say anything. My mouth is completely dry, or at least no sound comes out of it. The question is if I'm even breathing now. Amira does not have the same dilemma as I do, which is fortunate, and she responds quickly, "You have nothing to do with that." Amira turns to me, thus turning her back to the men.

"It's a shame for our people that you go around dressed like this," the man says angrily, almost screaming now. Both men leave us while they continue to speak in Arabic.

I can see that Amira's whole body is shaking and tears are running down her face. I take her aside and she explains what the conversation was about. Since she is already threatened by her father and brother, the men's attack raises a lot of emotions, such as her fear and desire to escape. After a while, Amira calms down, and we go in and sit down in the lecture hall to listen to the lectures. However, I am still very upset by the incident. Amira seems to have already overcome the worst, but I feel with all my heart that the interaction was completely unacceptable.

The two men sit a few rows ahead, obliquely to the left. When one of them turns around and looks back in the hall, I stare at him sourly. If only eyes could hurt, I think to myself. I tell Amira to stay where she is while I go and look for the person responsible for the conference. Science and research work are important global matter to protect, and nothing that should be harmed or limited by politics or religion. That's the whole point, after all. We do not come closer to people's equal values than at a scientific conference. At this conference, which consists of delegates mainly from all over Africa, everyone shares a common interest in analytical chemistry. Everything else, such as culture, religion, skin color or gender, does not really matter. What matters, however, is whether you can demonstrate high quality in your research.

With determined steps, I trot out through the hall to look for the person in charge of the conference. Fortunately, I have known the person for several years, since we were both PhD students in Lund in Sweden. I find him in a tent with refreshments, including a conversation with one of the conference delegates. He looks into my eyes and realizes that it's serious. The other person leaves the place discreetly.

"Nelson! Something totally unacceptable has happened!" I say, clearly upset, and do not pause for a second before continuing. "Two men have verbally attacked my postdoc, Amira. They threatened her. Maybe they will find out who she is and notify her father and brother," I say, shaking my voice. I make myself more and more agitated, I feel, thinking that I must try to calm myself down and take a deep breath.

"What exactly happened? What do you want me to do?" Nelson wonders calmly.

"In Sweden, Amira has protected housing, but now she is scared. Very scared," I say, much calmer now. It feels good to be able to tell this to a responsible person. Especially since I have known Nelson for many years, and I know that he knows what the right thing to do is.

"Do you want me to kick these men out of the conference? I can do that if you want," he says.

I think it would be the best thing really, but then I wonder if it will make those gentlemen even more disgruntled and then really hurt Amira. I suggest we go and talk to Amira together. We walk across the well-watered and well-trimmed lawns towards the conference room, and find Amira in the same place I left her. She follows us out and we talk through it all.

"I don't think you should force the men out of the conference, but ask them not to disturb me anymore. I don't want them to come and talk to me throughout the conference," says Amira.

She is so wise and so strong. I really admire her. It happened as she wished, and the men did not disturb her anymore. However, I stared angrily at them as soon as I got the chance. I insist that scientific conferences are a neutral and global arena where everyone can meet to discuss research results. Religion cannot and should not matter. No question about it!

Chapter Four

Firas's Story

Lund, Sweden, 2014

After two years of doctoral study, I was very frustrated with the results of my lab work and I had not yet been able to publish a scientific paper. The project that I was working on made me nervous and I began to feel that all the long hours that I spent working in the lab were for nothing. I had lost confidence in my abilities, and I began to think that I was not qualified for doctoral studies.

I had talked to Rawya about the problems and told her that I wanted to quit my doctoral studies. But she asked me to be patient when making such a decision and told me that she was confident that all problems would be solved and that things would go well. I continued my studies for a while, but I could no longer bear the pressure of working in the laboratory without achieving good results, which made me feel more nervous.

One day, as I sat in my office, overwhelmed by feelings of despair, I decided to abandon my doctoral studies. I sent an e-mail to Lotta and Maggan and asked for an urgent meeting with them. The next day, the three of us gathered around a small table in Lotta's office. I displayed signs of despair, with frustration and sorrow showing on my face.

"Oh, Firas! What's the matter with you?" Lotta wondered.

"It seems like something serious has happened!" Maggan added.

They were both worried.

"I want to quit my doctoral studies!" I announced.

"What?!" Lotta exclaimed. She and Maggan were both shocked by this news.

"Why do you want to quit your studies? What happened?" Maggan asked.

"I have been working for more than two years in the lab and I haven't had any satisfactory results, and I am starting to feel that I am not qualified to study for a doctorate. I can't bear the tension and the pressure any longer."

"Oh! So that's why! I thought for a moment that something serious had happened," Maggan said as she sat back in her chair, while Lotta leaned forward with smile on her face and said, "You're the classic Ph.D. student. Most doctoral students go through a crisis like this. It's normal. Don't worry, it will pass."

"But when I think about my project, I become very nervous," I tried to explain.

"So, don't think about it!" Maggan said and laughed.

"What?" I was puzzled.

"Yeah! I agree with Maggan." Lotta said. "Don't think about the project if it causes you tension. You need to take a week or more of vacation and try to stay away from the lab, your project, and anything else that causes you tension. Then, after you're relaxed, we can talk again."

I had a feeling of reassurance after this meeting, and I actually went on vacation for a few days. Then returned and requested another meeting with the two of them.

"I hope you're feeling better now and that you've changed your mind concerning your studies," Lotta said.

"Yes, I feel better now, but I want to change my project if you both don't mind."

I was afraid that they would reject my request, but their reaction surprised me.

"I have no objection, as long as it's what you want," Maggan said.

"I agree," Lotta said.

Their spontaneous response had a positive impact on me, and I was encouraged to take out some papers from my bag and put them on the table.

"Here's the project I want to work on!" I started to explain with renewed enthusiasm.

During my vacation, I thought about working on this new project. When I started my doctoral studies, Lotta asked me to be in charge of the installation of a new and modern instrument; an instrument that uses only so called supercritical carbon dioxide as a solvent. With this apparatus, I had already conducted a number of experiments on vitamin D and carotenoids in parallel to my doctoral project. In doing so, I had come up with many new ideas and I thought about pursuing them now instead of continuing with my original project.

"Now I can say that you're truly on the right track. The main purpose of your studies is to teach you to come up with new ideas and to learn to think independently," Lotta said.

Both welcomed the idea, but now I faced a new challenge: Time. I had to complete this new project in only two years, the remaining time on my scholarship.

***

Fall of Mosul
Iraq, 5th of June 2014

Since December 2013, the organization of the Islamic State in Iraq and Al-Sham (ISIS) had launched frequent attacks on bases of the Iraqi army and security forces located in western Iraq, specifically in Anbar and Mosul. On June 5, 2014, dozens of ISIS fighters launched a surprise attack on Iraqi forces in Mosul and bloody clashes erupted between them and ISIS militants over control of several neighborhoods in the west of the city, including Haramat, Mashirfa, and Tamoz.

I didn't expect these skirmishes with Iraqi forces to cause fall of the city so quickly. I thought that ISIS' control of some of Mosul's eastern districts was only a phase in another round of skirmishes that would end in their defeat, as we had seen several times before.

On June 6, ISIS seized another five suburbs on the west side of the city, and they attacked and burned the police station. The police and the army evacuated the western side of the city. In the beginning, there were less than 400 ISIS fighters, with about 100 vehicles, but after they entered the city, all the dormant ISIS cells in Mosul activated and thousands of militants joined their ranks.

On June 7, ISIS fighters advanced toward the Nineveh Hotel, which had been evacuated of all civilian guests, as the Iraqi forces continued their retreat. The battle at the Nineveh Hotel was the straw that broke the camel's back for the Iraqi army and police forces in the city. The attack on Mosul exposed the weakness of the Iraqi army and the fragility of its military and intelligence structure.

The fighting in Mosul continued until late in the day on Sunday, June 9, when ISIS targeted the Iraqi security forces with a truck bomb loaded with C4 explosives that exploded next to the Nineveh Hotel when many senior Iraqi military commanders were present. The tanker truck, loaded with explosives, headed toward the last line of defense on the right bank of the city of Mosul. The police and army opened fire, but the truck bomb managed to reach its target and exploded. After that, the western line of defense evaporated. The security forces collapsed, and Iraqi soldiers and policemen retreated toward Erbil and Duhok in Kurdistan, leaving their weapons and military equipment behind. The Iraqi high command in Mosul abandoned its headquarters and lost contact with the units deployed in the city's suburbs, which included field officers and soldiers. As a result, these units fled the city when they no longer received any orders to fight or retreat, resulting in the complete military collapse of Iraqi forces.

After five days of skirmishes between ISIS fighters and Iraqi forces, the terrorists now controlled the second largest city in Iraq. On June 10, 2014, the city of Mosul fell completely in the hands of ISIS militants. Several hundred terrorists had defeated and forced the retreat of Iraqi political and military leaders, along with their forces, estimated at nearly 50 thousand soldiers and policemen, all equipped with the latest weaponry. ISIS now controlled the city of Mosul, as well as its vital infrastructure, including the administrative center for the Nineveh province, the airport, and television channels. Their first official act was to release hundreds of prisoners from the Badush Central prison, the second largest prison in Iraq after Abu Ghraib, as well as those held in prisons at police stations throughout the city.

Columns of smoke rose from the police stations and former Iraqi army barracks. The dead bodies of Iraqi soldiers were publicly displayed on the five bridges of Mosul. Army and police vehicles were burned. The helmets and boots of Iraqi soldiers littered the roads, along with their military uniforms and weapons. Fires burned at several gas stations and checkpoints, and many people with their children filled the streets looking for help to take them by car to a safe place.

On that day, there wasn't a single soldier or policeman left in the city; everyone had abandoned their positions and fled, leaving behind empty army posts and police stations.

The number of people who tried to flee Mosul and enter the province of Duhok was terrifying. Hundreds of thousands of residents of Mosul attempted to reach safety in Kurdistan. The region was in complete disarray as refugees overwhelmed the Kurdish security barriers, where the check points were severe. The number of people displaced from Mosul was beyond imagination. Many of them were forced to return to Mosul either because they could not pass through Kurdish check points or under threat from ISIS that their property would be confiscated, or families harmed. At 3:00 pm on Monday, June 10, ISIS leaders showed their force by using Iraqi military vehicles in streets of Mosul.

***

Camp Speicher Massacre
Tikrit, Iraq, 12th of June 2014

Tikrit, which is close to Mosul, was no better off. ISIS quickly moved to Al-Shirqat in the Saladin governorate and occupied it, advancing to the outskirts of the city of Tikrit, 170 km north of Baghdad.

On June 12, there were more than 5,000 Iraqi Air Force cadets in Camp Speicher, a military base near Tikrit, 11 kilometers west of the Tigris River. Although threatened by the ISIS advance, Iraqi camp commanders — for reasons that are still unclear — ordered the cadets to take a 15-day leave to return to their families. The officers promised to provide them safe passage after ISIS seized Tikrit. They also ordered the cadets to leave their weapons behind and to take off their military uniforms and dress in civilian clothes for security reasons.

The cadets left the camp and, as they walked along the highway looking for a means of transport to take them to Baghdad, they were intercepted by several trucks and buses carrying ISIS militants. The ISIS terrorists separated out Shia and non-Muslim cadets from the Sunni ones. The Sunnis were allowed to go after signing a pledge of loyalty, while the ISIS terrorists seized the Shia and non-Muslims' shoes, rings, wallets, and identity cards, and they shot anyone who tried to hide their valuables. They then tied up them and loaded them onto the trucks and buses and took them at gunpoint to the Al-Qusour Al-Re'asiya region.

The ISIS terrorists then proceeded to kill the cadets, employing different methods. Many of them were shot, one at a time, and dumped in the Tigris River. Hundreds of them were forced to lay in mass graves in the desert and then were gunned down with automatic rifles by the militants, blasting them with a seemingly endless barrage of bullets to ensure that there were no survivors. Others were buried alive.

ISIS executed around 1,700 unarmed Iraqi cadets and announced to the world that the fighters of this terrorist organization were an enemy of a new type. Not only did they seek to seize and retain land, but they also wanted to eliminate their enemies when they fell into the hands of his fighters.

ISIS advanced rapidly toward Baghdad and seized control of two more cities just 65 km (50 miles) northeast of Baghdad, and then stopped for unknown reasons. The Iraqi forces formed a defensive belt called the "belt of Baghdad."

Kurdish forces, called "Peshmerga," took advantage of the massive collapse of the Iraqi federal forces in the region and quickly moved into the disputed areas, including Kirkuk, Sinjar, Bashiqa, Bahzani, and other cities, to fill the void.

On July 5, 2014, the Islamic State announced the establishment of the "State of the Islamic Caliphate" in parts of

Iraq and Syria, with its capital at Mosul, under the authority of its leader, Abu Bakr al-Baghdadi.

***

Lund, Sweden, July 2014

A few days after the fall of Mosul and other cities in Iraq, I met with Naseem and Abdulghani for coffee in a café in downtown Lund.

"How could the largest provinces in Iraq fall so quickly to a small group of terrorists? Especially compared to the size of the Iraqi police and army, which are all equipped with modern weapons and equipment?" Naseem asked.

We were all still in a state of shock over the recent events. We were concerned for our families living in Iraq because ISIS was now only 20 kilometers outside of Bashiqa and Bahzani.

"It's because of the sectarian tensions between Shia and Sunni that have erupted recently. People in these cities no longer trust the Iraqi army and police. It is the same for the army and the police — they feared the people would turn against them, so they threw down their weapons, took off their military uniforms, and fled," Abdulghani said.

"Although I still cannot believe what is happening, I think this is the result of the policy of the Iraqi Prime Minister, Nuri al-Maliki. People in our provinces no longer regard the army as an Iraqi army, but rather they call it the Maliki army," I added.

"That's true. Maliki recently dismissed many army officers from the Sunni sect and replaced them with others from Shia sect. Most of these officers didn't even graduate from military college, but they were from Shiite militias, opposed to Saddam Hussein's regime, who were based in Iran," Naseem said.

"ISIS took advantage of the anger and dismay of the residents of these cities due to repeated random arrests, and accused many people of these provinces who opposed to the government of terrorism under article four of Anti-Terrorism Law, which created a fertile ground for the terrorist groups to become active," Abdulghani said.

"Therefore, you find that this terrorist organization extended its authority and influence only in these cities, which were incubators for its inception and proliferation, but it stopped and could not expand beyond these incubators. It stopped at the outskirts of Baghdad and can no longer advance because there is insufficient support in Baghdad and southern Iraq. It also stopped on the outskirts of Bashiqa, Bahzani, Sinjar, and other cities inhabited by Kurds, Shabak, Yazidis, and Christians," I added.

"How is your family in Bashiqa?" Abdulghani asked me.

"They're fine. Yesterday I called my brother, Dilshad, and he told me that there were many Kurdish fighters (Peshmerga) in the city, as well as on the borders with ISIS. They dug trenches and erected earthen berms. What about your family?" I asked Abdulghani.

"They left Bashiqa from Duhok at the beginning of the ISIS advance, but they returned after knowing that there were large enough numbers of Peshmerga forces present on front lines to defend the city," Abdulghani said.

"My family didn't leave the city either," Naseem said. "Kurdish forces have asked the people not to panic, not to leave the city, and said that they will defend them to their last drop their blood."

"Do you think that the Peshmerga forces can hold off these barbaric terrorists?" I wondered.

"Yes, they will because the Kurdish army is a national army and has a great belief in its cause," Abdulghani answered.

"What if the Peshmerga can't hold them off?" Naseem asked.

We all panicked and sat silent for a moment, looking bewildered at each other.

"It would be a complete disaster!" Abdulghani said.

"They will slaughter everyone because they consider us infidels," I added.

Naseem took out his mobile phone and pulled up a map of Iraq on his screen.

"If ISIS attacks Bashiqa and Bahzani, they will surround the city and block the road that leads to Duhok, as well as the road leading to Erbil. Then only one road will remain for the people to escape from the city, which is the road through the mountain." Naseem said.

"But it is a narrow and winding road. If ISIS attacks the city by surprise, perhaps only a few will manage to escape using this route or by fleeing through the mountains. As you know, most people in the city, including my family, don't have cars," I said

"I think if they attack the city without warning, no one will survive because the ISIS fighters are only 20 kilometers away from Bashiqa," Abdulghani added.

"What about Sinjar?" I wondered.

Naseem looked for Sinjar on the map and when we realized its location on the map, we were all shocked. Sinjar was already under siege on all sides by ISIS fighters.

"If they manage to take Sinjar, there will be a bloody massacre!" I said.

***

After a few days, everyone believed that the advance had ended and that new borders had been drawn. Iraq was already divided into three regions: Kurdistan region, Sunna Stan region, and Shia Stan region. The Iraqi army and the Peshmerga forces dug trenches, erected dirt barricades, and took a defensive stance, while ISIS fighters stopped advancing, as if they were content with what they had gained. I remained in constant contact with my mother, my brothers, and my friends in Bashiqa and they told me that the life in the city was going on normally and that the situation was stable, and security was settled.

One day, I came home from work and, while we were having dinner, Rawya told me that her twin brother, Rouid, would marry in August and she wanted to attend the wedding. I told her that the situation is very dangerous in Iraq and it would not be wise to go there at this difficult time. She was also hesitant to go, but there was a kind of emotional and psychological bond between her and her twin brother. Sometimes they felt each other's pain. In rare cases, there is sometimes a state of telepathy where one can feel the feelings of the other, causing them to share pain and joy. She knew that not going there would cause grief to her brother. I called my father-in-law, my mother, my siblings, and several friends to check on the situation in Bashiqa. All of them assured me that life had returned to normal, and that security situation in the city was stable.

At that time, I was working on my new project and I was under a great deal of pressure. Time was running out and I was working late in the lab, often throughout the entire weekend.

"Well! Everyone seems to be safe in Bashiqa and things are fine in the city," I said to Rawya while we drank tea after dinner.

"Yes! That's true. I contacted my family and friends and they all confirmed this to me," Rawya agreed.

"But I'm afraid I can't go to Iraq with you."

"Why?" Rawya asked, clearly annoyed.

"As you know, I'm busy working on my new project and I don't have enough time to travel. I'm rushing to finish my studies before my scholarship ends."

"Well! I'll travel with the children," she said.

"I'm so sorry my dear," I replied. "But I wouldn't feel happy with all the stress I have here to finish my work."

"Okay, my dear! No worries!"

In mid-July, Rawya and my children traveled to Iraq, leaving from Copenhagen airport to Erbil where she was met by her parents and siblings. In the evening, she called me from Bashiqa. She was happy to be surrounded by her family and my family. She reassured me that everything was fine, and the situation was very calm and safe.

Chapter Five

Lotta's Story

Lund, Sweden, 25ᵗʰ of July 2014

It is Friday morning, almost 10:00 am. The sun is shining and it is a lovely Swedish summer. I look out through my office window, and I see a few hares with long ears jumping around on the lawn next to the parking lot. My window has lots of salt stains on the outside from all the rain from the winter and the early spring. Perhaps I should ask the janitors when it is time for window cleaning. Why am I sitting here in my office during my vacation? Why do I choose to work with a thesis manuscript on such a fine day? One of my doctoral students, Jiayin, will meet with me shortly to discuss a draft of her thesis. To be a teacher at the university is more than a job — it is a lifestyle, a passion for research and science. It is also a passion for teaching and supervising others. In fact, the biggest joy is to watch young people develop and learn to become great scientists and leaders. It is not so bad to be at work this day, I think to myself, when I see Jiayin just outside my office door.

"Is it 10 o'clock now? We have a meeting, right?" Jiayin asks.

"For sure," I answer. "Come on in! Or should we go and grab some coffee first?"

"I am okay, but if you want to have some…" Jiayin says politely

As we walk towards the coffee room, I ask her how she is doing now that she is close to the deadline for printing her thesis. She does not look that stressed, although in my opinion, she should be stressed. Most doctoral students are extremely stressed when time gets closer to printing their thesis and defending their research. If there is something I have learned as a teacher and a supervisor, all people are different. It is risky to make any assumptions. Jiayin simply is a person that does not easily get stressed. She is very calm despite the fact that within a couple of months, a so-called opponent will ask her lots of questions about her thesis for one or two hours in a public hearing. After that, an examining committee of three experts will ask even more questions. It is this committee that decides if the doctoral student will pass or fail. In a way, the whole doctoral thesis defense is quite dramatic. Sometimes it happens that the student gets so stressed that he or she cannot answer even the simplest questions. Then it is really important that the printed doctoral thesis is well written. It should be the doctoral student writing the thesis, and not the supervisor. I usually ask the student lots of questions during the writing process, and together we discuss the clarity of scientific questions, methods, and conclusions.

"How is the writing going?" I ask Jiayin

"It's going fine," she says, smiling at me.

"Have you seen my last comments on your work?" I continue.

"Yes, I emailed a new version to you last night," she answers

"Okay, I didn't see that. I will have a look," I say. "Let us go back to my office and discuss."

With the coffee mug in one hand and the door key in the other, I manage to open the door and we enter to sit down to talk about the progress in her thesis writing. Jiayin is a student from China, and she has done some really excellent research in my group, combining analytical chemistry with mathematical modeling; however, the writing is not going as well as the calculations and practical experiments in the lab. We discuss how to write the thesis to make the reader understand better what she has been doing and why, during her five years as a doctoral student in my group.

"So, when is the deadline for printing your thesis?" I ask Jiayin.

"The 11th of August," she says.

"Alright. Since I am on vacation now, send me a text message if you have emailed a new version of the thesis, in case you would like some more feedback on the text," I tell her.

"Thank you Lotta!" she says with a smile and leaves my office.

I am thinking about all other things I should have done at work before starting my vacation, but I didn't find the time for. Like preparing for the training course on the new equipment that we have purchased. Another even bigger worry is whether Firas will ever finish his bilberry project. Still, the manuscript is not ready to be submitted, and still some more experiments are needed to be done. Firas has more than one project now, but still… 'Why is it taking such a long time?', I am thinking, both a bit irritated and worried. It is my responsibility as a supervisor to make sure that he gets a good education and that he becomes doctor in philosophy. Maggan is the main supervisor, and I am the assisting supervisor. We are both supposed to be on vacation now. I sigh and stand up stretching out my stiff neck and back. I really do need vacation.

I look down on my desk at the fifth (or is it sixth?) draft of the bilberry manuscript. There are trolls in this paper, I am thinking. I grab the manuscript in my hand, and I decide to look for Firas. He sits in an office a few doors from mine, down the corridor. I find him by his computer, and he appears to be more stressed than usual. Between his eyes, I spot a deep wrinkle. He is completely focused on reading on his computer monitor.

"Hi, Firas! How are you doing? Is everything alright?" I ask him, while I sense that he is not alright at all.

I see that he is following the news on his computer about the ISIS activities in Iraq. Of course, he must be so worried about what is going on there. He has parents, siblings, and cousins there, as well as friends. I would be dreadfully worried too.

"I am worried about the situation in Iraq," Firas replies as if he is reading my mind.

"I also follow the news about ISIS. They should have been stopped long ago, already in Syria," I tell him.

"Did you know that I am Yazidi?" Firas asks, looking intensely at me.

"No, I had no idea," I answer him back, completely surprised and a bit shocked.

Until just a few days ago I had no idea that there is a group of people called Yazidis, or Ezidis. However, during the last few days in newspapers, different experts say that the Yazidi people are in great danger as ISIS is progressively taking over the northern parts of Iraq. That is, in even more danger than what has become the baseline for these people. Thousands of Yazidis have already been killed in Iraq during the last several years. Most news sites currently have facts about Yazidis, considering all the ignorant people like myself who have no idea about these people.

"I am so sorry Firas, I had no idea," I tell Firas with anxiety in my voice. "Is your family okay?"

"Yes, they are fine. ISIS has taken Mosul, but now things have calmed down," Firas says.

We bring up the map of Iraq on his computer for him to show me the locations of Mosul and his town of growing up, Bashiqa. I feel so uneducated and ignorant, not knowing these things about Firas. Even though he has been in my research group for several years, I did not know exactly where in Iraq he is from, and that he is Yazidi. I just knew that he does not mind drinking beer, and that he loves watching European football. I have also dealt with previous problems that I suspect were threats from Muslims in Lund. Someone cut off the cable to his computer mouse one day. Also, his wife has been threatened by another chemistry student at the Chemistry Center, who said that coming from Iraq and being a woman, she must cover the hair with an Islamic veil.

After a while, when Firas has told me more about his people and what they believe in, he tells me that his wife Rawya and their children had just for Iraq.

"Why? That sounds too dangerous," I tell Firas, shocked. "Why would she even consider going?"

"It's her brother's wedding," he answers. Firas also looks a bit worried, and I am thinking that this is the reason why he appeared to be so anxious when I first saw him here by his desk.

"Do you also have to leave? Maybe you can convince Rawya to return to Lund immediately?" I ask Firas, even more alarmed now, thinking about what could happen to her and their kids.

"She was determined to go there to attend her brother's wedding," Firas says.

"How will you even be able to focus on your research?" I am wondering.

I cannot prevent myself from thinking about his bilberry project, and the also on-going Vitamin D project. In just another year and a half, Firas should defend his thesis. How will this even be possible? What I like about Firas though, and also with most of the doctoral student in my group, is there is no problem to be frank and to use a very straight form of communication. Those who are not used to my straight way of talking do get used to it pretty fast. This is a way of avoiding miscommunication, and to save time. It could be embarrassing or shocking at first, but in the end, it simplifies things.

"Firas, how will you be able to finish your PhD degree on time?" I ask him straight, even though I know his mind is in Iraq now. "I've revised your last version of the bilberry paper, and it's right here," I tell Firas as I hand over the around twenty-page manuscript full with my handwritten comments in purple ink. I love using purple or pink ink, and I avoid red. Red is too dramatic. Black or blue is boring. Firas looks at me and says, "Lotta, I am not sure. I will not follow my wife to Iraq. Instead, I'll be staying in the lab and work hard to finish both the vitamin D project and the bilberry paper," he says.

"I'm not sure if you will be able to focus on this" I say. "Maybe it is better if you follow your wife to Iraq? What if the war gets more serious now?" I say, worried. "Family and health go before work, you know that, Firas. Right?" I tell him

"Yes, I know. Don't worry, the Kurdish Peshmerga soldiers are defending Yazidi cities. It should be okay," he says, trying to convince both me and himself.

Chapter Six

Firas's Story

Fall of Sinjar
Lund, Sweden, 2nd of August 2014
One day before the massacre

It was Saturday, and although it was a holiday, I'd been working hard in the lab. I stayed until late and at ten o'clock, I felt hungry and very tired. I went back to my apartment to relax, prepared my dinner, put it on the table, and then I had a video call with Rawya as usual.

"Hello, Rawya!"

"Hello, Firas! How are you?"

"I'm fine, my dear! And you?"

"I'm fine, and the kids are too! What are you doing?" she asked me.

"I'm having my dinner!"

"At this late hour?"

"What can I do?" I said. "I just returned from the lab."

"You should have come with us instead of exhausting yourself like this. Everyone here is asking about you. Your mother is sad because you didn't come with us. She misses you, but she is happy to have Maxim and Enana here."

"I miss her too and miss all of you as well," I told her.

"Maxim and Enana miss you too."

"So, tell me, how are the preparations for the wedding going?"

"Everything is complete. The wedding will be held next Thursday. Hang on a minute!"

Rawya went to another room and took out some clothes and said, "What do you think of this suit? I bought it for Maxim, and he will wear it at the wedding."

"What a beautiful suit," I commented.

"And this dress will be worn by Enana."

"Wow! It is very beautiful! She will be more beautiful than the bride in this dress. What beautiful clothes you've picked out for them. What about you?"

"I won't show you just now. You'll be surprised when I wear it at the wedding."

"I'm excited to see you wear it."

"You have to be patient!" she said, and she laughed.

"Where are the kids? I miss talking to them."

"They're asleep. They had fun and played a lot today."

"Well! Kiss them for me. I'm tired as well and I want to sleep."

"Okay, darling! Try to sleep well! I know that you haven't been sleeping well lately."

"Don't worry, I will. I'm going to put my phone on silent mode so nothing can disturb me. Good night, my dear."

"Good night."

I hung up the phone and finished my dinner and then took the dirty dishes and placed them in the kitchen sink. It was around midnight and, before I went to sleep, I remembered that I had left my phone on the dining table. I went back and placed it in silent mode and then set it on the table again. Then I went to the bedroom and lay down on my bed. I was so exhausted that in only a few moments I fell into a deep sleep.

***

Karzark, Iraq, 2nd of August 2014
The Karzark battle

On the evening of Saturday, the second of August, abnormal movements took place near farms and Arab villages surrounding Karzark, a small village inhabited mainly by Yazidis located south of Sinjar, about 20 kilometers from Mount Sinjar. The village was surrounded by a dirt barricades on all sides. It was guarded by the village men, who numbered less than 250 fighters, in addition to a few Pesh-merga fighters. Karzark was the first line of defense and a gateway to break into Sinjar from the south. The fighters stationed on the berms noticed dozens of ISIS's four-wheel-drive vehicles and Humvees, which have been seized when ISIS occupied Mosul, spread to the Arab villages and farms surrounding the village, not more than 2 kilometers away.

When these cars arrived in these places, they turned off their lights. There was a state of anticipation all throughout the evening until 2:00 am of 3rd August. At approximately 2.30 am, an attack began, as ISIS fighters raided the village, firing mortars from the neighboring Arab farms and villages, which killed many of the residents in the village. Their forces advanced and began to fire heavily in the village. The Yazidi men fiercely defended their village but could do little as they watched the mortars fall on the homes of their families.

It was an unequal battle in terms of weapons, equipment, and the number of fighters. Still the men of Karzark fought bravely. The battle continued until 3:30 am. The villagers managed to burn and destroy many ISIS cars and kill many terrorists. After nearly an hour and a half of fighting, the ISIS fighters retreated, but the villagers began to run out of ammunition.

The villagers, mostly women and children, fled toward the mountain. Many of them had to flee on foot for lack of transport, while most of the men defended the village. Thousands of Peshmerga troops were located less than 10 kilometers from the village, and they had promised the inhabitants of Karzark that a large force would join them in the event of an attack. The village men contacted the Peshmerga forces and informed them that they were under attack and that they didn't have enough ammunition to hold out. The Peshmerga forces replied that additional troops, ammunition, and equipment would arrive in less than half an hour. The villagers waited impatiently for assistance from the rear lines but to no avail. No response had been received from the leaders of the Peshmerga forces. The Yazidis had placed their trust in the Kurdish security officials, but at this critical moment, they let them down. They didn't send arms and ammunition to the villagers to help them to defend their land and their families. The Peshmerga forces didn't fight, and they were the first to flee the area with their military vehicles through Syria.

***

At around 4:30 am, terrorists resumed their attack as reinforcements had arrived and they reorganized their ranks. The men of the village continued to defend their village, hoping Peshmerga reinforcements would arrive, as well as providing cover for their families to escape from the village. The Humvees began to advance as the villagers fired off their remaining bullets into the vehicles until their ammunition ran out. Many villagers were killed, but a few managed to escape. ISIS fighters stormed the dirt barriers and occupied the village, which was almost empty. One of the Yazidi women, carrying her small son on her shoulder and holding on to her little daughter's hand, tried to escape the village on foot, but a shot from one of the Humvees shattered her daughter's skull. The mother began to wail and fell to the ground as well, but she had no choice but to get up and carry her little son toward the mountain, leaving the lifeless body of her little daughter behind. The cars and the Humvees with ISIS terrorist didn't stop in the village but moved on directly to Sinjar.

With ISIS advancing, the Peshmerga forces withdrew from Sinjar, leaving the unarmed civilians to face their fate. Sinjar is an Iraqi city located in the western province of Nineveh in northern Iraq, close to the mountain of Sinjar, and 80 kilometers away from Mosul. It is inhabited by a majority of Yazidis, with a population of more than 350 thousand inhabitants.

With the collapse of the resistance in these areas, ISIS fighters broke into about 40 cars in these villages, killing all the men, women and even children on their way. When news of the genocide reached Sinjar, the situation collapsed even before the arrival of ISIS terrorists.

***

"Yova" The Little Girl

Yova woke up to the sound of mortar shells and bullets flying overhead. Yova was a little girl, only six-years-old. What were her wishes before she closed her eyes on that fateful night? What did she dream of before she woke up, frightened and putting her hands over her ears to drown out the sound of the shells exploding around her?

Her parents awakened the rest of the family and carried their children in panic to escape the grip of the ISIS fighters who were on the outskirts of their small village. Both her father and mother made sure that all the members of the family rode in the back of their pick-up. Among the passengers were other families who had no means of transportation and who rode with them. The truck became overcrowded. The father sped off toward the mountain, while the mother, who sat in the back of the pickup, grabbed on to her children for fear they would fall out. Yova sat next to her mother and held her tight, filled with fear as she cried. Yova was unaware of what was happening around her, why they were fleeing, from whom, and to where.

The father drove the pickup quickly along the unpaved road, and in his side mirror, he could see the lights of the distant terrorist cars as they came closer and closer. He sped up to reach the entrance to the mountain to seek shelter. One of his tires struck a small stone, which threw the vehicle off balance. At that tragic moment, Yova couldn't hold on to her mother anymore and fell from the truck. Her mother tried to reach out to grab her little girl, but she couldn't catch her. Yova fell screaming "mam…!" She couldn't finish the word because of the speed of the pickup. The mother screamed hard "Yova … Yova…" and everyone yelled Yova as they pounded on the roof of the car to tell her father to stop. The father realized that his little daughter, Yova, had fallen, but he continued driving toward the mountain.

"Why don't you stop? Didn't you hear them yelling that Yova has fallen? We should stop to pick her up," his brother, who was sitting next to him in the front, said, crying and screaming.

"I want to stop, but I can't. If I stop, they'll take us all," the father said, shedding tears.

He looked through the side mirror to see if he could spot his daughter, but she disappeared in the darkness of the night and the rising dust, which was punctuated by the lights of the vehicles carrying the ISIS terrorists who were chasing them.

The mother tried to jump out to go after her daughter, but the others grabbed her and prevented her from doing so. She kept reaching out for her daughter, screaming, and weeping "Yova… Yovaaaa… Yovaaaa…"

***

The horror of the massacres and the suspicious with-drawal of Peshmerga forces from their positions in the city ended any possibility of resistance in Sinjar. The road to the mountain was flooded with families seeking shelter there, while others fled to the Kurdish cities of Duhok and Zakho, and to the Syrian border. Hundreds of other families were unable to leave because they had no cars, or they had sick patients or elderly people who could not walk. These people were the first victims of the ISIS terrorists. Within hours, dozens of men were killed, and hundreds of women were taken to the Islamic State detention centers in Baaj, Tal Afar, and Mosul.

Before dawn, one could see the terrifying sight of an endless stream of car lights stretching from the edge of the desert winding up the mountain. These vehicles carried tens of thousands of panic-stricken people seeking refuge in Mount Sinjar. And as the first rays of the sun peaked over the horizon, groups of families, exhausted from walking, who did not find vehicles for transportation, also reached the entrances to the mountain. The worried eyes were moving quickly between the visible distance of the rocky mountain and the road leading to the stricken city, checking every newcomer for fear that they would be ISIS fighters.

Hours later, thousands of families clambered along the mountain paths, consuming the energy and strength of the elderly and the children among them. They gathered near the mountain grooves, which provided some shade to reduce the heat of the burning sun, while sounds of gunshots could be heard in the distance. Tens of thousands scattered to every available spot as they awaited their fate. Either Kurdish Peshmerga forces would arrive to save them, or the terrorists would launch an assault on them. The latter seemed increasingly likely, given the surge of bangs coming from the outskirts of the city.

Stories of mass murder and assaults on girls began to spread quickly through mobile devices that did not stop transmitting the shocking news. With the complete disappearance of the Peshmerga forces, following their total withdrawal into Syrian territory, everyone realized that they now faced another massacre, to be added to the previous 72 massacres that the Yazidis had documented in their cultural heritage and epic songs. The families fled deep into the mountain and prepared for a battle with death in this harsh mountain, which is considered the last refuge, as it was during all the previous massacres. Everyone sheltered there was surrounded atop the mountain as the ISIS terrorists cut off all the routes leading out into the world. They had two ways to survive amidst the horrors they faced, either to die on the mountain of starvation and thirst, with temperatures soaring above 45°C, or to become easy prey for the terrorists.

During the early hours of the Islamic state's control of Sinjar, the terrorists ordered those who could not escape the city, by loudspeakers, not to leave their homes, assuring them that they were safe. Of course, the inhabitants did not believe them, but there was no way to escape. ISIS fighters killed every Yazidi man they encountered and took the women into the slavery.

Within hours, the bodies of dozens of men, while defending their daughters who had been taken as slaves, were randomly executed or killed, piled up in the streets.

Sinjar was the first home of the Yazidis and their last resort, but today it was an empty town with dead bodies scattered along its roads, and spread throughout the paths, streets, and alleys, while vehicles of the Islamic Caliphate State carried hundreds of her children sentenced to death to their mass graves, while the processions of enslaved women emerged from afar as they left the city on their way to terrorist strongholds.

***

Lund, Sweden, 3rd of August 2014

On the morning of August 3, my cell phone — that I had left on the dining table before I went to bed — started ringing, but I didn't hear it because I had put it on silent mode and I was still sound asleep in my room. But I suddenly woke up when I heard my doorbell ringing insistently. I got up from my bed and hurried toward the door. When I opened it, I was surprised to see Abdulghani standing in front of me at this early hour of the morning.

"I tried to call you several times, but you didn't answer." Abdulghani said, who lived nearby in the neighborhood, about a 10-minute walk from my apartment.

I could see that he had run all the way because he was breathing rapidly, which only served to increase my anxiety. I looked at him shocked, and answered:

"It's on silent mode. What's the matter?"

"ISIS attacked Sinjar."

Abdulghani knew that my wife and my kids were also in Iraq and that they were in danger, so he had rushed to my apartment when he failed to reach me by phone. I ran to grab my phone and Abdelghani followed me inside. I checked it and found several missed calls from my wife Rawya, Abdulghani, and other friends.

"The news from Sinjar is that many people have fled to the mountain and ISIS fighters are killing anyone they encounter in the city," Abdulghani explained as I tried to call Rawya.

"Hello, Rawya! where are you now?"

"Firas! ISIS attacked Sinjar and they are killing the men and abducting the women and children," she said, screaming and crying in panic.

"You must leave the city immediately and go to Duhok as soon as possible."

"But I do not have a car. My father's car has broken down and Rouid is trying to fix it."

"Calm down! And stay close to the children. I'll call my mother and then call you back again."

I hung up the phone and called my mother, who was also crying.

"You must leave the city immediately. Have you managed to find a car?"

"Yeah! A minibus will come to take us to Duhok now."

"Great, that's good. I will tell Rawya to bring the children and go with you."

I phoned Rawya and told her to go to our house. She grabbed the children by the hand and ran toward our house, but when she arrived there, my mother was crying in panic and told her that the driver was unable to come, and that they didn't have a car anymore. She called me again and told me about this. She was terrified and confused and did not know what to do.

"Rawya! Rawya! Calm down. Calm down and listen to me carefully. You have to go back to your parents' house now, and if Rouid has managed to repair the car or has any other means of transport, go with the kids immediately. I want you to stay in the street and keep eyes on our house because I will try to send a taxi from Duhok or Erbil to take you and my mother and brothers to a safe place. If you see a parked car in front of our house, go there immediately."

"Okay! Okay!" Rawya said, although she could hardly breathe.

"Calm down please! I know it is a very dangerous situation, but I'm relying on you in this critical time. Listen to me carefully! If things get worse and you cannot find a means of transportation, take the children and head for the mountain, and never stop. Understood?"

"Yes! Yes! understood!" Rawya said as she tried to regain her composure.

I asked Rawya to give the phone to my mother so I could talk to her.

"Listen, Mother! I will call a taxi. If things get worse, then do as I said to Rawya. Run to the mountain and do not stay in the city."

"Okay, son!" My mother said as she was crying.

I tried to keep control of myself and not to show them my own concern and feelings of panic. Abdulghani was in contact with his family and relatives in Bashiqa. After that, I quickly managed to book an airplane ticket to Erbil; the date of the trip would be on the 6th of August.

***

Northern Iraq, 3rd of August 2014

Around 1:30 pm, Rawya's brother managed to repair the car and Rawya fled Bashiqa with the children to Duhok. The car was packed with passengers. In addition to Rawya and the children, Rawya's mother, her three sisters, and two brothers were also in the car. Her father decided to stay in Bashiqa. On the way, the car broke down again. Rawya and her family were panicking and kept looking in the direction of Mosul, fearing of the arrival of ISIS terrorists. Rouid pulled over on the side of the road and managed to repair the car once more and then continued the way to Duhok.

My mother and my siblings managed to escape from Bashiqa at around 4:00 pm, after I was able to send a car through the mountain, which took them to my sister's house in Shariya, a town in Duhok inhabited by Yazidis. Rawya, my children, my mother, my siblings, and the inhabitants of Bashiqa and Bahzani all managed to escape through the mountain just hours before the occupation of the city.

Rawya, her family, and other families, found a small house in Duhok consisting of three rooms where they could take shelter. There were more than thirty people in this small house, but they were lucky because many other families couldn't find any shelter. Many of them scattered throughout the streets, parks, and schools because there was no place to shelter them due to the mass exodus of civilians toward Duhok from the cities now occupied by Islamic State.

The Peshmerga forces were still stationed on the border of Bashiqa and Bahzani. By the dark of night, the inhabitants deserted the towns, except for a few men who decided to stay and support the Peshmerga forces defending the city. But at around 10 pm, the Peshmerga forces began to withdraw from the front lines toward Erbil and Duhok, and the remaining men of the city left with them. Bashiqa and Bah-zani were now completely uninhabited. The city was abandoned to ISIS terrorists who entered the city without fighting. The Peshmerga forces, who promised the city's inhabitants to defend them to the death, fled without shedding a single drop of blood, and didn't fire a single shot from their rifles, the barrels of which remained cold despite the summer heat.

***

Lotta's Story

Lund, Sweden, 3rd of August 2014

What should not happen, happened. ISIS attacked the city of Sinjar in northern Iraq, and murdered thousands of Yazidis. Every hour I follow the news and the progress of ISIS and the inability of the rest of the world to do something. For some reason, everyone is waiting for the U.S. president Barack Obama to drop bombs over ISIS in northern Iraq and hope that this will put an end to the massacres and the jihadist war.

I become quite active on Facebook and Twitter, and I follow a journalist, Mr. Barber, who is reporting from inside Iraq. This man feeds Twitter with several updates per hour. It almost becomes toxic. I am so worried about Rawya and the children. I cannot imagine what Firas is thinking right now. I sincerely hope that he does not decide to travel to Iraq now. That should not be possible though, since there could not possibly be any flights going there.

***

The next day I meet an extremely stressed Firas in the research lab at work. His lab bench is full of volumetric flasks, dirty beakers, printed raw data, pipet tips, gloves, etc. It looks like he is trying to do research, but that he is failing. His face is stiff and his eyes are wide open. I can see that he is in a state of shock.

"Firas, what is going on? I heard the news yesterday. What are you going to do?"

"I'm leaving in a couple of days to Iraq! I need to bring my wife and children back to Sweden," he says with a strained voice.

"Okay, I understand. This sounds very dangerous! Can't you help them to get home from here?" I ask him

"No, I need to go there" he says with tears in his eyes.

I realize that there is no point discussing this further. I am thinking that he might get killed in Iraq together with his family. On the other hand, I would have done the same for my family. It is for sure difficult to just stay home and wait, and to be so far away from loved ones. Since I am a very pragmatic person, I am thinking that Firas will not be able to complete his bilberry paper now, even though he needs it so much for his thesis. I am also thinking about the collaborators we have at the medical faculty. They are waiting for the new analysis method for vitamin D. I ask Firas, "Do you have a backup of all your data somewhere?"

"Yes, I do a backup every day," he answers

"Can you put your backup in a Drop Box that I can read?" I ask him, "Please, just do this before you leave. This way, I can try to help you with your writing while you are away."

"I will take care of it," he says, without convincing me that he actually will do so. His mind looks like it is already in Iraq.

***

Firas's Story

Lund, Sweden, 5th of August 2014

As soon as he heard that I was going to Iraq, Abdulghani came to my apartment around 8 pm. I had just finished packing my small carry-on bag with only necessities.

"What time is your flight?" he asked.

"At two in the morning."

"So why are you leaving so early?"

"I can't wait at home any longer," I told him. "It is easier for me to wait at the airport."

I threw my small bag over my shoulder and we left my apartment together and walked to the bus station nearby.

"ISIS has occupied Telkif, Bartella, and other cities around Bashiqa, and has advanced very close to the Mosul Dam. Maybe they will occupy it today," Abdulghani said.

"Yes, I know. ISIS fighters advanced towards Makhmur and Al-Kuwayr, less than 50 kilometers from the center of Erbil. If ISIS manages to take control of those two cities, they will cut the road between Erbil and Duhok."

"If ISIS occupies these two cities, the road to Erbil will be open and Erbil may also fall," Abdulghani added.

"What a calamity! I'm afraid that my trip to Iraq might be cancelled if the situation gets any worse."

"What's your plan?"

"I'll go to Iraq and bring Rawya and my children back to Sweden as quickly as possible."

"You know that the situation in Iraq is very dangerous and by going there you'll put yourself at risk too?"

"It doesn't matter! What kind of life would I have if something happened to them? I'm going to be with them, either we live together, or we face the death together."

The bus arrived and I said goodbye to Abdulghani and set off for the Copenhagen airport. The hours of waiting at the airport seemed like years and I closely watched the flight board for fear of cancellation. I also kept a close eye on the news and remained in contact with my wife and my mother.

Finally, the long-awaited moment came, and the plane took off to Erbil. Tired and exhausted, I look out through the airplane window as we leave the ground, thinking that I'll bring my family back to Sweden.

Chapter Seven

Around 7:00 am in Iraq, my plane landed at the Erbil International Airport. As soon as I got out of the airport, I called my wife and told her that I was now in Erbil and that I would go directly to Duhok. Then I called my mother, but she didn't answer. Next, I called my brothers and none of them answered either. My anxiety increased greatly, and I was scared. I kept trying to contact them, but without any response. After several attempts, my young brother Dilshad replied:

"Hello Dilshad! Why don't any of you answer my calls?" I asked frantically.

"Firas! ISIS has occupied villages near Sharya, and they are on the outskirts of the city. We all fled towards Duhok and no one remained in the city."

I was shocked and panicked when I heard this news because it meant that Duhok was going to fall too.

"And where are you now?"

"We are homeless now. We fled hours ago from Sharya and we don't know where to go."

"Be careful and stay together. Don't split up. I am now in Erbil and I will come to Duhok. Send me the address of where you are now."

"Yes, I will send it to you immediately, but I don't know if we will stay here or keep on the move."

"Just let me know where you go."

***

Getting a taxi or any other means of transportation to Duhok was not easy. Everyone was afraid to take the road between Erbil and Duhok, especially since ISIS fighters were on the outskirts of Makhmur and Al-Kuwayr and there was a strong possibility that they would capture those two cities today or tomorrow. I was standing in the public transport center with another group of people who also wanted to go to Duhok. All the drivers refused to go there until I and three other men persuaded a taxi driver to go after we offered him a large amount of money. The driver agreed and we immediately set out for Duhok.

The driver tried several roads but most of them were blocked by either dirt or concrete barriers. In a moment of despair, the driver decided not to go to Duhok and to return to Erbil, as he lost hope of getting through with all the roads barricaded. We begged him to keep trying, and then one of the passengers suggested that the driver take another road he knew, but the driver replied that the road was far and potentially blocked as well. We begged him to try this road one last time and if it was closed, we would return to Erbil. The driver headed for the proposed road that fortunately was passable.

Halfway to Duhok, we came across a wave of refugees. Hundreds of men, women, and children filled the road, while hundreds or perhaps thousands more were coming from Makhmur and Al-Kuwayr. They were accompanied by many soldiers who tried to control security and organize traffic, but their efforts were vain. Our car came to a halt, along with the other cars on the road, creating a massive traffic jam. The driver then asked one of the refugees:

"What's going on?"

"ISIS has occupied Makhmur and Al-Kuwayr and is on its way to occupying Erbil as well," the man who had escaped from ISIS replied. "People fled in different directions, but they all aimed to get as far away from ISIS as possible."

The women carried their small children on their shoulders, the older ones running behind their mothers with the mid-day sun beating down upon them, and the temperatures reaching more than 45 degrees Celsius. The men carried on their backs whatever food and drink they could gather before they fled their homes. Many lorries and bulldozers accompanied the refugees as they fled and helped them to reach safety. The soldiers tried to direct the traffic and open the roadway to end the traffic jam. Little by little, we made our way through this mass of humanity fleeing ISIS terror. I saw in the faces of the displaced women the face of my mother, my wife, and my sisters, and in the faces of the frightened and tired children crying in dismay, I saw the faces of my own children and those of my brothers.

Before I arrived in Duhok, I called my mother to ask where they were now. She told me that they had fled to yet another place, this time because of the hot sun. They had taken shelter in one of the alleys. I knew where it was because I had lived in Duhok for more than three years while I was working at Zakho University. I called Rawya and told her the whereabouts of my mother and my brothers, and I asked her if she could reach them so we could all meet there. Fortunately, she said "Yes! I can."

***

When we entered Duhok, I looked out the window to find large crowds of people filling the streets, parks, and under the bridges. Before I reached the city center, the driver stopped the car and one of the other passengers asked him, "Why did you stop here?"

"Don't you see the chaos and the traffic jam?! I'm afraid if I keep driving towards the city center, we'll get stuck in the traffic. I brought you to Duhok as we agreed. Now you have to manage on your own from here!" The driver said nervously; he just wanted to get out of there and a dispute started between him and the other passengers, but I didn't wait around. I just opened the door and got out of the car.

The streets were filled with people going in all directions. I had to make my way through this huge crowd to cross to the other side of the street, which passed by the Duhok market, and then from there I could get to the place where my family had taken shelter. There were many men carrying light machine guns, some of them in military uniform, but many others in civilian clothes. As I walked through the crowd, I saw many pick-up trucks that were slowly maneuvering through the crowded street, carrying armed men in the back as well. Some of them climbed down from the pick-up trucks in the Duhok market, while others remained in the backs of the pickups. The situation was chaotic, and I didn't know whether these gunmen were fleeing the battlefield or on their way to the front. Loudspeakers broadcast Kurdish national songs from all the shops on both sides of the street to inspire the spirit of citizens and fighters.

***

When I managed to get out of the crowded Duhok market, the traffic became less congested. I flagged down a taxi and asked him to take me to the military district where I was supposed to meet my family. When I finally arrived there, I found many displaced people filling the streets and side-walks, most of them sitting in the shade to take shelter from the heat of the sun. I looked at all the faces, searching for my wife, my mother, or any other member of my family. I knew many of the people there as most of them were from Bashiqa and Bahzani. I asked someone I knew from Bashiqa if he had seen my family and he answered, "We were all together in Sharya, but when ISIS approached the city, we fled here and dispersed, but I glimpsed your mother and your siblings at the end of the street."

I thanked him and made my way down the block where I found my mother sitting in the shade and leaning against the wall. She put my little ten month old nephew, Mohsin, on her lap. She was very sad, holding a piece of cardboard in her hand, moving it as a fan backwards and forwards in front of the child face to make him more comfortable in the heat. As I ran towards them, my sister, Sondos, saw me and started screaming my name, "Firas! Firas!" My eyes kept searching for my wife and children as well. My mother raised her head in amazement and looked around her. When her eyes fell on me, she gave the little child to his mother, who was sitting next to her, and she got up and quickly ran towards me.

We hugged each other and wept. I almost fainted from the heat and emotion. I lost my strength and could no longer stand on my feet. For the past few days, I was nervous and worried that I wouldn't see any of my family members ever again, so I barely slept. I couldn't believe that I was embracing my mother once again, and I fell to my knees from intense weeping and fatigue. I put my hands on my face and I just sat and cried. My mother and my brothers all huddled around me and we hugged each other as tears streamed down our faces. I didn't know why I was crying so much. Was it out of joy because I found my mother and my brothers safe? Or I was crying out of sadness because I found them sitting in the street, homeless? Or was it out of fear for all of us because ISIS fighters had penetrated the outskirts of the city and we didn't know where we would escape to this time?

I got up on my feet and continued to look around for my wife and children, but I couldn't find them. Then I asked my mother, "Where are Rawya and the kids?"

"She called me just a few minutes ago," my mother told me, "and said that she was on the way here."

Meanwhile, Rawya held the hands of Maxim and Enana as she made her way through the throngs of people. When she finally saw me, she started screaming, "Firas!" I turned and ran towards her and we hugged each other as we cried. Maxim and Enana also hugged me, crying.

***

More than an hour had passed, as I sat with Rawya, my mother, and the rest of the family on the street. Enana sat in my lap complaining about the intensity of heat, while Maxim nested himself between me and his mother and rested his head on my arms. He was exhausted from the heat as well. Rawya looked at me, worried, and asked, "What are we going to do now?"

"We have to get to Erbil and from there we go back to Sweden, but first we must find safe shelter for my family." I said in a matter of fact tone.

As we talked, my sister, Sondos, told me that she had received a call from one of her friends telling her that there was a storage unit at the bleach factory where we could hide. The storage was abandoned and belonged to a man from Duhok who opened its door to displaced families. We made our way there, along with a few other families.

"Have you brought your passports?" I asked Rawya.

"Yes, they are with me."

"Ok! Good! We have to go to Erbil now."

"Now? What about our families?"

I had no answer to this question. I looked at my mother and the rest of my family as they sat on the floor of this abandoned warehouse, filled with the smell of bleach and detergent.

"I don't know!" I answered. Still looking at my mother, I added, "I don't know that by staying here can help them much but remaining here is a danger to us and children. We must return Maxim and Enana to Sweden."

My mother noticed that I was looking at her and she approached me and said, "What are you going to do now?"

"I don't know! But I told Rawya we need to return to Sweden."

"Yes, my son! You have to leave this place as soon as possible and to save yourself and your family," she said.

"But what about you?" I asked with worry.

"Being here with your family increases my anxiety and fear. Don't be afraid for us."

"Ok! We will sleep here tonight and tomorrow morning we will go to Erbil," I said.

***

We said goodbye to our families. It was a sad farewell as we had no idea if or when we would see each other again. Then we left the storage facility, Rawya and I, accompanied by Maxim and Enana, and began to look for a car to take us to Erbil. We stood on the street for a long time, but we couldn't find any car to take us there. All the drivers refused to go to Erbil because all roads were blocked. The streets remained crowded, and the sight of armed men roaming the streets only added to our fear and anxiety.

Finally, I was able to convince a taxi driver to take us to Erbil, although he told us that it was almost impossible under these circumstances. When we arrived at one of the checkpoints, we were surprised by the long line of cars, as well as the hundreds and possibly thousands of men, women, and children, waiting to cross. After more than an hour of waiting, the driver began to fidget and said, "I cannot wait any longer. We have no hope of getting through. I will go back to Duhok."

I thought if I would leave the car with my family and wait with the others, maybe we could pass through the checkpoint, but I abandoned this idea because I learned it was dangerous to cross on foot, especially since I didn't know how long it would take to pass through the checkpoint, or even if we could get through at all. I didn't know what would happen or come next. I was still in Duhok and the road to Erbil was long and fraught with danger.

"Okay! Could you please take us to Zakho, on the Turkish border?" I asked the driver, in the hope that I could cross into Turkey. From there it would be very easy to return to Sweden. I kept insisting and the taxi driver finally agreed after I offered him a large sum of money because the journey to the Turkish-Iraqi border would take more than three hours.

We arrived at the border, the situation there wasn't any different. Thousands of displaced people waiting at the border to cross into Turkey, and I was disappointed to learn that the border was closed for security reasons as well. The sun was about to set, and I asked the driver to bring us back to Duhok. After this day long adventure, we returned to the storage facility. My mother and my siblings were very sad because they knew why we had come back — there was no way out.

***

That night, I sat with my family in the storage facility. We were all filled with great fear and anxiety. Villages and cities are falling one after the other to the ISIS terrorists who were moving rapidly toward Duhok and Erbil.

"Oh my God! Help us! We are trapped in this city," my mother said, as she was crying.

"I heard that ISIS is just 20 kilometers away from Duhok. What if they enter the city?" Rawya said, as she trembled with fear.

I grabbed Rawya's hand, trying to calm her down, and I told her, "We are together now." Then I looked at my family and added, "We are close to the mountain. We need to prepare bags with water and food. If ISIS storms into the city, we will flee to the mountain. We have no other choice."

My older brother, Fares, added, "We must remain vigilant as well as stay in contact with others in Duhok and Erbil. I agree with Firas, we have no other solution but to escape to the mountain. We must take turns standing guard during the night."

***

Because of the extreme heat and suffocating atmosphere, fraught with fear and anxiety, I was exhausted from
fatigue and it had been several days during which I hadn't
slept for more than two hours continuously. Rawya asked
me to sleep a little when she saw how exhausted I was. She
was also exhausted. We had nothing to sleep on, so we
spread some cardboard boxes on the ground and slept on
them.

I didn't sleep well. I had the most horrifying and vivid
dream that ISIS fighters had broken into the storage facility
while we were all asleep and started shooting at the walls
and roof of the building. We all woke up scared, children
and women screaming and crying out of fear. Rawya
grabbed my arms firmly as she cried, while Maxim and
Enana hid behind us, screaming and crying too. The terrorists opened fire on two men who tried to resist and killed
them, while several them went and captured the women and
children. My older brother, Fares, tried to stop one terrorist,
when he grabbed his wife, but they shot him and killed him.
My mother ran and threw herself on my brother and she was
crying, while the blood was running from his body. I was
screaming and standing in front of my wife and children trying to protect them with my body, then several other terrorists approached me. I tried to resist them, but one of them
hit me with a bottom of his rifle on my face. I fell to the
ground and blood ran from my nose. I lifted my head to find
them dragging Rawya, my mother, my sisters, my sisters in
law and all the children and women out of the storage.

Maxim and Enana screamed as they reached out to me for help, but I was unable to do anything. I tried to get up, but I couldn't. I watched a terrorist with long and ugly beard drag Rawya by her hand as she was screaming, crying, and asking me for help too, while the other ISIS fighters executed the remaining men. I screamed loudly:

"Rawya... Mother ... Maxim ... Enana ...

Then Rawya awakened me up from my nightmare.

"Firas! Firas! wake up!"

My body was sweaty with the heat and fear of this nightmare, and my throat was dry too. Rawya gave me a bottle of water to drink, and she asked me:

"What's wrong, dear?"

"Nothing. It was just a bad dream."

"Ok! don't worry! Try to sleep again."

"I cannot go back to sleep, dear. I'll go take the guard duty to relieve my brother Fares. Good night."

"Good night."

Rawya returned to sleep while I went to sit with my brother Fares, who was on watch with another man. I asked Fares to go to sleep because I would replace him and keep watch instead. I had quit smoking more than five years ago, but I felt a great desire to smoke a cigarette when I saw the other man smoking. I asked for a cigarette and lit it. Then I started blowing smoke in the air and I began talking to him.

"What city are you from?"

"From Sinjar."

"Were you in Sinjar when ISIS attacked the city?"

"Yes."

"And where's your family now?"

"They're here with me. My wife and three children, two boys and a little two-year-old girl."

"And how did you manage to escape?"

"We arrived in Duhok after we fled the death trap on Mount Sinjar, and we are overcome by exhaustion and hunger."

His name was Shammo, a shepherd who grazed his sheep in the pastures surrounding Sinjar. Shammo and thousands of others had fled during the past few days from the western side of the mountain, crossed plains and hills to the Syrian border, and then returned to the Kurdistan region of Iraq.

"When we climbed to the top of the mountain, snipers shot at us. I was with my family and my mother, an elderly woman. ISIS militants captured thousands of our women and children and killed the men and every boy over 13 years old."

He remained quiet for a few moments and took a deep drag on his cigarette, exhaled it with sorrow, and then continued, "I left my mother on the mountain in a cave. I begged her to let me carry her on my back, but she refused and told me that she wanted to remain there. Save yourself and your family."

Then he began to cry like a child and wiped away the tears pouring out of his eyes. I couldn't help myself either, and I cried. Shammo continued to talk and said, "I stayed for two days on the mountain with my family, waiting for someone to save us. There were thousands of us. More than fifty graves were dug, and bodies buried in them, mostly small children who died from hunger and thirst. One pregnant woman and her fetus died during the ascent up Mount Sinjar, seeking safety from the ISIS terrorists. Our suffering increased during the night, especially as we listened to the sound of the children crying from hunger and thirst. In the daytime, our work was limited to burying the dead and searching for sources of water and any plant we could eat.

The words seemed to stick in the man's chest, and he began to cough. I gave him some water and he drank a little and then continued his story, "Those who come down from the mountain still have to cross a dangerous area before reaching a safe place. Despite the suffering on the mountain, tens of thousands of people still go there because their lives are in danger. Thousands of families, mostly elderly people, are still trapped on Mount Sinjar because ISIS control the road linking Sinjar to Duhok and Erbil. We were trapped between the hammer of ISIS and the anvil of hunger, thirst, disease, and bad weather. We have taken the road between the Syrian-Iraqi border and Al-Malikiyah city, also called Dayrik, inside Syria. Along the dirt road that crosses the border between Iraq and Syria, one could see an endless stream of refugees crawling on foot under the blazing sun and through dust storms. After hours of hard walking, with intermittent breaks, we arrived in Dayrik, and from there we went to Duhok."

I looked at him sadly and tried to tell him something encouraging, but I couldn't find any words because I was as frightened, frustrated and filled with despair as he was.

***

The next day, as I sat on the ground in the storage building, feeling desperate and frustrated, I looked at the empty cardboard pile placed in one corner of the building. At that moment, I felt more worthless than those boxes. They were at least valuable to someone who had carefully placed them in the building. I felt like no one cared about me or my family.

All of our attempts to get out of Duhok were failing. We felt like mice stuck in the trap. We flopped in all directions to escape this trap but to no avail. There was no escape. It was an insulting feeling. I had run out of solutions. What was this feeling of helplessness? Was it the end? At that moment, it seemed that we would need a miracle to get out of the city. Our survival depended on the Peshmerga forces resisting and preventing the terrorists from storming the city

Last week, I was studying at one of the best universities in the world, and my dream was to finish my studies and go back to work in my country. Now I am stuck here with my wife and children in Iraq. Outside, terrorists pursued us, intending to kill me, and to enslave my wife and my children. Despair overtook me. The sense of helplessness was killing me, and in a moment of desperation I decided to send a message to Lotta and Maggan. I had lost all hope and realized that everything had collapsed and ended.

I sent the SMS and threw the phone to my side and then I went back to look at the cardboard boxes again.

Chapter Eight

Lotta's Story

Lund, Sweden, 8th of August 2014

It feels like a long time ago since Firas left to save his wife and children from ISIS in Iraq. I have no idea how it is going. I have no idea if they are still alive. All I can do is to follow the news. I am very grateful to Mr. Barber who is constantly reporting via Twitter from the Mosul area of northern Iraq.

In Sweden, the summer is very hot, unusually hot. I spend my vacation days gardening, as well as preparing for a keynote lecture that I will be giving in Durban next week. It is an international conference on green chemistry, which had been planned since the year before. While I am sitting in the kitchen after a full day in the garden, my phone declared with a beep that I have a new text message. I read the SMS sent from an international phone number that I did not have in my address book. My heart beats faster, and my whole mind focuses on this one text message.

Dear Lotta and Maggan. I'm Firas Jumaah and this is my phone number. Now I'm trapped in Duhok with my family due to the ISIS took over my city and all Yazidis places. Another piece of bad news is that the ministry of higher education told me that they don't have money and they have no idea when they can pay the family allowance. As you read this, I understand if you can no longer be responsible for my PhD education. If I am not back in Lund within three weeks, then please remove me from the PhD program. Regards, Firas.

I am shocked to read this on my phone, but still relieved to hear some sign from Firas; he is still alive. I was thinking that it must not be possible to operate phones properly in a country in war. I answer him back right away:

We will never stop your PhD study! You are a PhD student forever until you get your degree. Thank you for sharing your phone number! I have been thinking about you all day. Obama has started bombing in the north. Perhaps he can put an end to this disaster. Please keep us updated. I am so worried. Let me know how I can help!! Provide with news from outside? Regards, Lotta.

My answer to Firas came rapidly, spontaneously and directly from deep in my heart. I have a similar feeling as the one that flowed through me when Amira was verbally attacked by the two Muslim men at the analytical chemistry conference in Maputo. First, I am shocked about the whole terrifying situation, but a few seconds later, I am angry. Why would I stop Firas's doctoral education? That will not happen! In fact, it is stated in the Swedish Higher Education Ordinance that all doctoral students have the right to defend their thesis to become doctor. This means that Firas has his legal right to defend his PhD thesis, and it makes me angry that ISIS can come in and put an end to it. Politics and religion should not tamper with the integrity of academic freedom. This is an opinion that I strongly believe in. For some reason, this is important to me. Perhaps this is what defines me as a Professor. On top of being angry about the fact that somebody caused Firas to think that he could no longer be a doctoral student in Lund, I am also extremely worried about the whole escalating situation in Iraq. Firas and his whole family could get killed any hour from now.

I read Firas message again, and I realized that I had only partly answered his message. I send another message:

> I will talk to Maggan and Ola about the financial situation. I am sure that we can solve this.

Directly after sending the message, I press "call back" on the phone. I do not care how much this would add to my phone bill. I need to hear Firas's voice. My hands are sweating, and my mind is filled with stress that feels like a flickering of thousands of greyish particles. I cannot notice the everyday activities going on around me in the kitchen. Kuria is preparing dinner, Gabriel is playing with the rabbit, Stampe, and Elias is doing something in his room. Maybe playing with Lego. It is six o'clock in the evening, and the sun is still shining outside. At this time of the year, the sun doesn't set until around nine o'clock in the evening. I can sense the smell of barbecued meat. Lamb perhaps. Everything is so trivial compared to what is happening right now in northern Iraq.

"Hello?" Firas says from the other side of the world.

I am surprised that someone picked the phone, and that someone is Firas, my dear doctoral student. It is amazing how crystal clear the sound is, even though there is a war happening in the background.

"Hello, Firas, this is Lotta," I say with stressed and anxious voice.

"Hello, Lotta," Firas answers with a weak voice.

I can hear that Firas is sobbing now, and neither of us says anything for a while. I am thinking that right now, I am no longer just a supervisor. From this moment, I am a personal friend too.

"Where are you now? Are you safe?" I ask Firas after a while.

"We are in a warehouse, an abandoned building. My whole family is here," Firas tells me.

In those few words that Firas tells me, I can hear so much more than only what he actually says. His voice unveils that he has lost hope, that he has given up. Misery, fright, despair. This explains why he suggested that I stop his doctoral education.

"Firas, don't give up," I tell him. "There has to be a way to get you out of there."

"I don't know," he says. "All the roads are closed, there is no way out."

We are both quiet for a while, and Firas continues, "I will see what is possible. Maybe we will have to escape through the mountains."

"That doesn't sound safe at all. I hear on the news every day now people getting killed in those mountains," I tell Firas with my anxious and sharp voice.

We continue talking for a while. I try my best to cheer him up, and to be that solid rock in his life that he so desperately needs right now. We agree that we should stay in touch by text messages over the phone. Very stubbornly, he says that every now and then, he takes pictures of his surroundings with the built-in phone camera. I sharply tell him that it is a very bad idea to walk outside taking pictures when ISIS is so nearby, just a few kilometers from there. At a distance over the phone, I can hear sounds of bombs. Firas explains that it is probably Obama trying to help now, by dropping bombs on ISIS strongholds. I am thinking that at least the U.S. has a great president now in Barack Obama. After all, his ancestors are from Kenya, just like my husband.

As we hang up, I can hear that Firas´ voice sounds a little bit more hopeful. I call Maggan to tell her about what is going on, and what we can do to help Firas. Maggan is away on a wrestling competition with her two children. We talk for a long time on a noisy phone line as she is sitting in a sports center. In fact, the noise is so much worse than the sound transferred though Firas's phone in Iraq. The despair I can hear from Maggan's voice is almost as bad as what I just heard from Firas.

While having dinner with my family, I talk to Kuria about the extremely difficult situation for Firas and his family. It is so comforting to hear my husband's very pragmatic attitude about pretty much anything in life. After talking with him, I realize that of course it is possible to help Firas and his family to escape from the ISIS fighters in Iraq!

***

Later that night, I am in bed with my cell phone in front of me. I read updates from Mr. Barber about ISIS frightening progress northwest of Mosul. I find some absolutely terrifying news on Swedish radio also; "Right now: The U.S. is attacking ISIS in Iraq." I open Facebook and post a link to this news with a status update for my friends in Swedish, perhaps just to relieve some pressure from my mind:

> The whole thing is very miserable! One of my doctoral students has traveled to Iraq to save his family. Now they have moved to Duhok in northern Iraq by the mountains. I hope everything goes well!!! There are mass executions in the area, completely insane.

It doesn't take long before I see a comment to my post, written by my schoolfriend Hedvig. We were neighbors, as well as classmates from grades four to nine. Back then, I lived in a city called Gävle, which is along the east coast of Sweden. Hedvig used to love to dress up in colorful and funny clothes, play theatre, and pretend to do interviews using a skipping-rope as a microphone. Today she is a successful journalist at a national radio station in central Sweden, in a city called Karlstad.

> Ugh, how awful! Where did his family live? Are they Kurdish? Do they belong to any religious minority?

I answer Hedvig, thinking that she must also be following the news carefully, since she is a journalist. It's likely that most journalists around the world are following the situation in Iraq.

> In the Sinjar region. My doctoral student is Yazidi and it's not so good in this situation. It's never been easy for him. Strong guy. I just hope he manages to escape out of the country and back to safety in Lund!

Hedvig and I continue to write each other messages though Facebook. It is a relief in a way to have someone to communicate with about this war and the situation for people fleeing from Iraq.

> Hedvig: Poor guy. It is deadly dangerous in Northern Iraq now. Imagine traveling from safe Sweden down to that hell. What a hero!

Lotta: Absolutely! His wife and children went there several weeks ago, so in this case it was pretty obvious. It's hard to imagine his situation. In addition to executions, there is a shortage of food and water, and according to my doctoral student, they fled to the mountains and live in caves...

Hedvig: Yes, I've read about it. 200,000 people flee ISIS and many of them hide in the mountains where they have neither food nor water. But why did his wife and children go there?

Lotta: A relative is getting married next week so the reason for the trip was a wedding. But I also find it a little strange. I guess you can have the homesickness even though there is such unrest in the country.

Hedvig: Yeah, sure. They might not understand that this would happen either. Have you had phone contact with him?

Lotta: Yes, I have his contact number in Iraq. He will try to keep me updated.

Finally, long after midnight, I put away my phone on the bedside table and I try to sleep. Kuria is already fast asleep, but in my head, thousands of thoughts succeed each other, one by one.

∗∗∗

Lund, Sweden, 9th of August 2014

Saturday morning. I am restless, and I cannot do anything to help Firas right now. First thing on Monday morning I will talk to human resource personnel at work to see what we can do to help him. I spend the day inside the house doing laundry, cleaning the rabbit cage, making pancakes for my boys, and other small everyday tasks to keep my thoughts away from ISIS and Iraq. Of course, it does not work. My mind is all the time with Firas. I am so worried. In the evening, I send a text message to Firas:

> Firas have you managed to leave the mountains with your family? Is your family ok?? Regards, Lotta.

After waiting for 15 to 20 minutes for a reply from Firas, I start worrying even more. Did anything happen to him? Did ISIS enter Duhok and captured him and his family? Or is the phone just switched off? Finally, two hours later, I receive a reply from Firas:

> Dear Lotta, thank you very much for your kind words. Don't worry we haven't been in the mountains because we managed to escape from our city a few hours before ISIS entered. Now we are in a safe place, but we don't trust people around us. Regarding the financial issue, we've agreed that I'll finance my PhD study and I should respect this agreement. Although we are in miserable situation, I am looking to the happy side that all my family (my mother, siblings, brothers, and sisters in law and our kids) have managed to survive and we are all together in

the same place. This smile is for you :) My top priority is to evacuate my wife and kids out of Iraq. I really appreciate your SMS and it's very kind of you. Warm hugs, Firas.

I feel extremely relieved, and I answer Firas immediately in case he will quickly switch off his phone again:

Thank you, Firas!! That was very good news!! I hope that you can put your family in a safe place or bring them all to Sweden! The rest we will solve when you are back. You are a hero! ;) Regards, Lotta.

***

Lund, Sweden, 11th of August 2014

It is Monday morning, and I try to hurry up a little extra with breakfast and getting ready for work. I know that this day will be a very long day considering everything I would like to achieve. It's already eight o'clock in the morning and the sun is warming. I get on my bike with the red saddle with white spots. While biking to work I think about the phone call I received from Hedvig yesterday. After our communication via Facebook she contacted a journalist at a national radio program in Malmö, which is a major city just south of Lund. They are working colleagues, but just operating from different parts of Sweden. Hedvig told the journalist in Malmö about Firas being trapped in Iraq with his family. She also told her that I am in phone contact with

Firas. So now this journalist sincerely wants to do an interview about the situation in Iraq. There are extremely few sources of news from inside of Iraq, and none from any Yazidi trying to hide from ISIS. This would be a unique broadcasting from the inside — but perhaps also dangerous for Firas, I am thinking while I rapidly bike uphill towards the Chemistry Center in Lund. All I could promise Hedvig and that other journalist is that I will ask Firas what he thinks. Would he be willing to give this interview? Or should I not even ask him, and take the negative decision for him? Often, Firas is too generous for his own good.

I am extremely sweaty when I reach the Chemistry Center and lock my bike in front of Entrance A. Instead of going directly to my office, I walk to the administration part of the building where human resource personnel is found. Already by the entrance door to the administration corridor, I see through the glass window that HR personnel is there this early Monday morning. Administrators are not as lazy as researchers, I am thinking while I use my card key to get into the corridor.

"Good morning! How are you?" I say pretty loudly to Gunilla, the responsible personnel administrator.

"Good morning, Lotta!" she replies and she looks curious at me sort of waiting for a continuation.

"I have a problem, or rather, my doctoral student has a problem," I tell her with uncertainty in my voice. My whole body likely expresses uncertainty.

"Come in," Gunilla says and invites me to sit down in front of her desk.

Her office is fairly large and has a comfortable seating area on the side. The light flows in from a large window just above her desk. Gunilla is around 50 years old, and she has been personnel responsible as long as I can remember. I always liked her. She seems knowledgeable and concrete, and her communication skills are very straight, just like mine.

"So, what kind of problem is your student having, and who is this student?" she asks me.

"This is about Firas Jumaah. He is not an employed student, but rather paid by a stipend from Iraq," I tell Gunilla since she has already started to look for him on her computer. She will not find him since he is not employed, unless she looks in the database of admitted doctoral students.

"Okay, so what is the problem with Firas?" she asks me now.

"He went to Iraq to save his wife and children from the ISIS troops and the war going on there. Now they are all trapped there. The roads are closed. On top of everything, Firas doesn't have any money," I tell Gunilla with my worried voice. "Do you have any idea how I can help him?" I desperately ask her.

"Have you talked to the Security Manager here at Lund University?" she asks me

"No, I have not. Who is it and how do I reach him?" I ask with some new hope growing inside of me.

Gunilla tells me about the Security Manager, Per. While we talk, I remember who Per is. I have seen him many times in the basement and different hallways here in the Chemistry building. He is a tall man with wide shoulders, short grey-brown hair, a fairly large moustache, and spectacles. He is always carrying an earpiece, constantly ready to answer his cell phone. In the coffee room, people make jokes about him, saying that he pretends to be James Bond, waiting for something to happen in the boring hallways of Lund University buildings. It is a bit sad that people try to make fun of him. In a way, I can understand that there is not so much excitement in being a security manager inside the Chemistry Center.

I decided to send an email to Per, explaining the whole situation and the help I need from him:

Dear Per. One of my doctoral students (Firas Jumaah) is trapped in Duhok, Iraq. Firas belongs to the vulnerable Yazidi minority in Iraq. He left Lund on Wednesday to try to save his family from ISIS, and they have now been hiding in an industrial premise somewhere in Duhok. Now I need advice on how we can help Firas (and his wife plus two young children) to get back to Sweden. They are not Swedish citizens. Firas has half of his doctoral education remaining. If we manage to get Firas home with his family, then the question is whether he can feel safe and secure in Lund, given that he belongs to a minority and that there may be Muslims in Lund who do not appreciate Yazidis. Perhaps I should add that Firas is on a fellowship, i.e. Iraq pays his doctoral education, but no longer since the war started in Iraq. Now we plan to employ Firas on my research funds. Best regards from Charlotta Turner.

After about one hour and a half, Per writes back to me:

Dear Charlotta. I will ask a question to our procured personal protection if anything can be done. Hopefully, I will get answers tomorrow. Sincerely, Per.

I thank Per, and I also immediately inform my boss Ola as well as the head of the department of chemistry, the economy responsible and the personnel responsible. They all receive an email about the situation, in which I explain the situation for Firas and his family, being trapped in an abandoned factory in Duhok in northern Iraq.

Hello! Maggan's and my doctoral student Firas Jumaah is in an abandoned factory in Duhok, northern Iraq, where he has taken his escape with his relatives from ISIS. Firas traveled to Iraq last Wednesday because his wife and children were already there since earlier this summer. Maggan and I now need some advice on how we can help Firas. Iraq will not pay more for his doctoral education. Can we employ him using research funds? He has two years left, approximately. Then we also need help concerning how to send money to Iraq so that Firas can buy plane tickets for himself and his wife and children, when the situation has calmed down in Iraq.

Maybe External Relations at Lund University can help? Another issue is that of his safety, even when he comes back. I have no idea how sensitive this is; Firas belongs to a minority in Iraq. I think of ISIS terrorists in Sweden — maybe they are in Lund too? It shouldn't be any danger, but you never know! I have contact with Firas almost daily by phone. He is ok, and everyone in his family has managed so far. Problems that arise are around food and water. Now we can only hope that this comes to a happy ending! Regards, Lotta.

Now, I have started helping Firas and his family. I have engaged all key people I could think of at Lund University. Today is the day when Jiayin will print her thesis, but I cannot really focus on that. The adrenaline levels are high in my head, and it feels like I am operating at double speed. I send a text message to Firas to ask him about the radio interview:

Hello, Firas. A journalist at the Swedish national radio in Malmö would like to do an interview with you, to hear how you are doing, i.e. your story. It is a good opportunity. The radio lady wants to call you today... I can explain to you how she knows about you. Nobody knows your name though, and you should remain anonymous. Regards, Lotta.

I then call Firas to again hear his voice, and I explain the whole story with my friend Hedvig and the messages on Facebook, and her colleague at the radio station in Malmö. Firas agrees to do the interview, but he will not mention his name. He prefers to be anonymous, which makes sense.

Firas is careful, but still he would like the outside world to find out about the life for Yazidis in northern Iraq. Such a brave man he is, Firas! He also tells me about his life in Duhok now. The situation is hopeless, with a lack of food and water, and constant shootings and bombing in the background. What is also worrying is that it sounds like the forces are coming nearer to where Firas and his family are hiding. All of the sudden, the call was cut. I send and SMS to Firas:

> The call was cut. Stay safe and take care!! Next call is from the journalist at radio P4 in Malmöhus! ;) Warm regards from Lotta. P.S. Remember that what you are doing is so much bigger than a PhD degree!!

Firas send a message back to me immediately:

> Dear Lotta. It is OK and I believe that this interview will be useful for all families (more than 500 000). Maybe in this way I can contribute in helping them. Although my story is not sad in comparison to thousands of other stories, but still, I can explain how my family and more than 800 000 Yazidis are living in different places in the north of Iraq as homeless, in schools, and in factories with very limited food and medical care. Now I am in Duhok and no one knows where we will be in a few days. Thank you Lotta. Regards, Firas.

One of the most powerful means to take you anywhere, at any place in the world, is money. My next point on the Plan of Action is to help Firas getting some money in an account that he can get access to in Iraq. I send him a message asking about when he received his last payment, and information about his bank account. Firas answers right away:

> Dear Lotta, the last time that I had my family allowance and tuition fee was 2013-10-01. This is the only way to escape from here. About the radio, I told the journalist to keep my name hidden. I appreciate what you are doing for my family. You are my angel! Thank you so much. Regards, Firas.

I get emotional when I read this message. First of all, why is there so much pride about receiving or not receiving a stipend? Why didn't Firas tell me a long time ago that he no longer receives any scholarships? Maybe this is about a man being capable of feeding his family, or a man sticking to initial agreements. I have no idea, but I completely disagree. It would have been better if he already October last year had informed me and Maggan about the new situation about the lack of funding from the Kurdistan Regional Government. I send another text message to Firas:

> You have not had salary since last year?? My gosh, Firas, you should have told me! I will speed up the employment process! Which one of the Yazidi angels am I? ;) Regards, Lotta.

Firas texts me back informing me about his previous salary and why he had not received any payment from the Kurdistan Regional Government. Obviously, since there is a war between ISIS and the Kurdistan region, all scholarships were cut. Maybe I should have figured this out by myself. Well, I didn't. Firas tells me that he has not been able to pay his rent in Lund, since his bank account is on minus. He ends his SMS by telling me how I make him feel valuable for someone and that "before your text messages, phone calls and the radio interview, I felt that I was nothing in this world." My heart is crying for him.

I spent the rest of the evening thinking about practical things, such as how to finance the new employment of Firas, and whether we could employ him with a starting date several months back in time. For sure, this is not how it is supposed to be done. For a fact, we can only help Firas to get back home to Sweden if he is employed at Lund University, and he should have been employed already when he left for Iraq. It is not sufficient that he is a doctoral student on a stipend. Another fact is that Firas has not received his scholarship from Iraq since October last year, and by rules at Lund University, this means that we should have arranged his employment already! We would have if we had known about it. So, the most logical solution is to backdate the employment letter several months earlier. This is perhaps a slight bending of the rules, but I am happy to do this for Firas. The question though is how much bending of rules my line managers are willing to do.

After reading some emails, and hearing from my doctoral student Jiayin that the printing of her thesis went well, I go to bed exhausted. I had completely forgotten about Jiayin's thesis!

Maxim and Enana in Bashiqa in 2014, a few days before the genocide

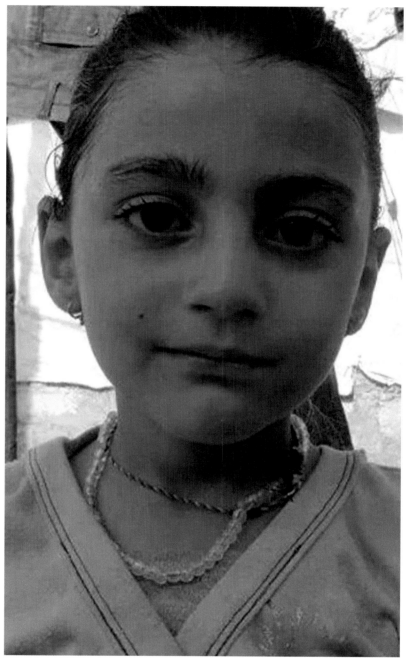

Yova, an innocent young girl from Sinjar, a victim of the genocide

Outside the storage facility (left), August, 2014

Inside the storage facility in Duhok, August, 2014

Firas, with Enana, Maxim, his nephew Mohsin and neice Sandra

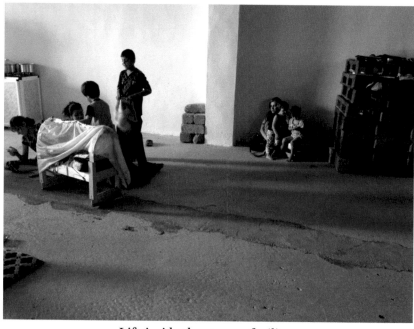

Life inside the storage facility

Firas's sister Sondos with Maxim (left), Enana (right)
and his nephew Mohsin in the storage facility

Per Gustafson, Chief of Security at Lund University
Photo by Robert Olsson

From left to right; Firas, Maggan Lotta, and Rawya in 2015

Dr. Charlotta "Lotta" Turner
Professor at Lund University, Sweden

Photo by Anna Thorbjornsson

Rawya, Maxim. Enana, and Firas
at Enana and Maxim's birthday party in 2015

Firas, with Enana and Maxim, nailing his thesis in 2016

Firas at his PhD dissertation defense on 29 April 2016

Firas's Ph.D. party, 29 April 2016

Charlotta Turner (Lotta) and Margerata Sandahl (Maggan)
at Firas's Ph.D. party

Firas receiving a F.C. Barcelona jersey as a gift
from his colleagues at his Ph.D. party

Maxim playing in a soccer match, Lund F.F., 2018
Photo by Erik Östergren

Maxim at Lund F. F. 2018
Photo by Erik Östergren

Chapter Nine

Lotta's Story

Lund, Sweden, 12th of August 2014

I woke up to the scent of fried eggs from the kitchen. It is omelet on the breakfast menu today! Hurray! Kuria is in full action in the kitchen frying mushrooms, onions and eggs. The buttery smell makes my mouth water.

"Please add some cheese to the omelet," I beg my dear husband.

"Good morning," he answers with a big smile.

I brew a cup of tea, and while waiting for this extraction process to complete, I fetch the newspaper from the mailbox outside our house. We are probably one of a few neighbors that still has a physical, cellulose-based newspaper. With the newspaper under my left arm, a plate with steamy omelet in my left hand and my cup of fresh Earl Grey with lots of milk in my right hand, I manage to enter the garden without dropping anything on the way. I find a nice sunny spot in a wooden chair with a comfortable seat cushion. We have a

brand-new wooden deck next to the house wall in the garden. This morning the sun is shining and it is calm. It's only
seven in the morning, and it's already twenty degrees Celsius in the shade. It will be a hot day, again. I open the morning newspaper and see the top headline: Robin Williams has
committed suicide. He suffered from depression due to his
dementia. So sad. The Ebola epidemic is still spreading in
West Africa, especially in Liberia. Imagine how frightening
it must be, not knowing if you are the next victim of this
dreadful virus! The forest fires are raging in Sweden and
hundreds of people are evacuated. Terrible! Turkey has a
new president, Recep Tayyip Erdogan. That is not good
news. Hillary Clinton, former U.S. Secretary of State and po-
tential presidential candidate, blames the ISIS terror group's
emergence in Iraq and Syria for what she calls President
Barack Obama's failed Syria policy. Nowhere in the newspaper is there any information about what is happening
right now in northern Iraq. How far has ISIS advanced? I
will check for new posts by Mr. Barber at Twitter.

As I finish eating my omelet and continue drinking my
tea, Kuria shows up at the doorframe.

"Is it good?" he asks me.

"Mm," I mumble back. "How can we sit here in the sun
enjoying an omelet when ISIS is killing people in Iraq? It's
completely absurd. And why don't the newspapers write
about it?" I continue, irritated now.

Kuria looks at me a little worried, "How's Firas doing? Have you heard more from him?"

"No, I haven't heard anymore, but I'll talk to him later," I say. "The omelet was good by the way. Great."

A wasp is buzzing over my plate, lands, and starts a cleaning process. The scents in the garden are fantastic. Soil, black currant bushes, apple trees with soon-ripe apples, a cherry tree, and a variety of small strawberry bushes. I wonder how Firas is doing, being so far away from here. Firas may be trying to help his wife and other families with breakfast. But just a couple of miles away, bombings are going on, and ISIS is advancing ever closer. A completely meaningless war is ongoing. What's the point? I'm not particularly interested in politics. Even less of religion. However, I have a belief. I believe in man, humanism, and equality. I also believe in science. Science has clear laws, and new hypotheses can be ratified by practical experiments. I think that being a researcher and a teacher is the best job you can have! I love my job! I get to meet people from around the whole world. In fact, although I am a chemist — an analytical chemist, to be more specific — I am more interested in people and the world around us. Societal development and cultural values are really interesting! The combination of natural science, engineering and social science is what keeps me motivated as a researcher. As a professor, I get to guide young researchers to become strong and independent in their profession. I also get to teach young students, and make them more interested in a subject — whatever the subject is. I love to see a lecture room filled with students, especially if they all look clearly awake! Another favorite part of my job is the queue by the coffee machine. It gives me an opportunity to have small fights, jokes, and chats with my colleagues. Another one of my favorite things about my job are the spontaneous research meetings taking place in the hallways or in the coffee room. The best ideas come from those impromptu meetings.

I think about all the interesting scientific discussions I have now and then with the doctoral students in my group. Recently, I've had a lot with Jiayin. While thinking about this, I clean after my breakfast, disappointing the wasp, and I get ready to leave for work.

By my office desk I start by checking the morning emails. There is one from the head of the department reading:

> Hi, Lotta. There is one thing to consider in this case. If I understand it correctly, Firas's trip to Iraq cannot be considered a business trip. So, he is not in a formal sense on a business trip (at a conference or something). One might put it this way: what *could we do*, what are we *allowed to do* and what *should we do*, as an employer? I have asked our Gunilla to find out more about this. Sincerely, the head of the department.

Immediately after I have read this email, I realize that this could mean trouble. I need to find a way to convince my bosses of the right thing to do. What we should do. That is, to employ Firas with a starting date several months back, and then to help him back from Iraq even though this was not a business trip. Hopefully, this is at least close to what we are allowed to do. The only way forward is to talk to the personnel administrator, Gunilla, to see what rules there are to bend, at least just slightly, and how to make the situation at least a bit better. I call her on the work phone.

"Hello Gunilla, this is Lotta" I say with my most enthusiastic voice. It is amazing how far you can get just by using positive thoughts and a happy and energetic voice.

"Hello Lotta" she says. "How are you?"

"Fine, thanks. I'd like to talk to you about Firas now. Can we arrange a doctoral student employment for Firas? He has not received any scholarship in 10 months." I say quite firmly on the phone. "We would need to arrange with this quickly now, since Firas is completely broke and stuck in Iraq with his family. Without money, it is hopeless to arrange a car to be able to escape, for example. Or to buy food for the family. How fast can this be arranged?" I wonder worriedly.

"Oh, this I can arrange with during the day. However, it must be decided by the dean. I will see if he is in. If so, I can hear if we can make a quick decision on this, maybe already tomorrow. Then there will be a few days before the salary is paid, but I can hear with the salary office if we can hurry!" says Gunilla with a calm and confident voice.

It's so nice to have this solid and trustable personnel manager! In addition, Gunilla is a person who sees opportunities a bit outside the box. It is not an overly common feature of administrators, and rightly so.

"Thanks, Gunilla, that sounds great! Will you let me know when the employment is arranged? I think it is needed before I can contact Per about whether we can help Firas and his family."

I hang up and I walk over to the lunch room to have my first cup of coffee of today. That is always the best coffee every day; the first one in the morning. Usually, I take the time to talk to people in the lunch room, but today, I feel too restless. Also, there is hardly anyone in the lunch room. Most people are still on vacation. I bring my cup back with me to my office. I cannot focus on anything except the progress of the rescue of Firas. I decide to call the head of the department.

After a few seconds of polite introduction, I ask what he thinks is allowed or possible to do for Firas. He tells me about his view on the situation, that we should probably do something for Firas, but we need to stay on the right side of the law. An important step is to have Firas employed, and then I should talk to the security manager. It would however be best if Firas was able to make his own way back to Sweden, if he could find a way to return to Sweden without any engagement of the security department here at the university. If there is no other solution, we should try to help, somehow.

The whole speech given by the head of the department on phone sounded quite uncertain, or vague, which is not surprising, because something like this has never happened before. Never before has a doctoral student or other employee been stuck in the middle of a war. Never before has Lund University had to start a rescue operation to bring an employee back home to Sweden. Sometime is the first time, I think. Now we are there. Now is the time to see what the university is going for.

I interpret the head of the department's whole message over phone as a green light, as long as I manage to get Firas employed. Also, my closest line manager, Ola, is fine with this. Quite satisfied with that, I check in on Jiayin how she is doing.

"Hello soon to be Dr. Jiayin," I say with a loud and clear voice by her office door.

"Hello," Jiayin shouts, as she was completely frightened by my sharp voice. She was in the middle of proofreading some of her printed thesis.

"Will the thesis be fine?" I ask her

"Yes, but some figures don't look so good," she says worriedly

"OK, it is common for this to be the case when printing. Check all figures carefully. Tables can also be printed incorrectly." I say with my supervisor voice. It feels great to let go of the worry about Firas.

"Did you bring lunch?" I ask.

"Yes," says Jiayin.

"Should we have lunch together? I can buy something in the Thai wagon," I say.

"Yes, absolutely. We can meet in the lunch room around 12," says Jiayin and I smile happily.

I return to my office and pick up my purse. I always keep it locked away in one of the wooden jalousie cabinets inside my office. On the way to the Thai wagon, my cell phone rings. Someone is calling via Lund University's switchboard, or it might be a forwarded call from my office landline phone.

"Charlotta Turner," I say with my authority voice.

"Hi, this is Per, security manager at Lund University," I hear a rough voice say with equal authority.

"Hello," I say and stop completely in my walk. With concern in my voice, I ask if he has found out more about how we can help Firas.

"We can help Firas and his wife," he said. "Did you say that they have children also?" Per wondered

"Yes, they have two young children. Around 3 and 6 years old," I tell him.

"Okay, so we can help the four of them to get out of Iraq. What we cannot do is help others in his family, like parents, cousins, and so on," he continues.

"Lund University has a contract with a security company that handles various assignments related to security. For example, personal protection. Or to arrange a secret home. Or, like now, to help someone back to Sweden from abroad. It may be because of natural disasters, or as in this case, a war. Although it never happened before from what I know. I don't think Lund University has helped anyone out of a war," Per tells me objectively.

"Okay, so how will this work out? How can we use the security company?" I ask.

"The security company, in turn, has contacts, subcontractors, you could say, all over the world. I've looked up Iraq, and there are three or four different companies there that we can use. These are like taxi services, though with a much higher security level," Per says as if we are talking about ordering pizza.

I'm totally amazed. Could this be true?! It seems that there is a well thought out routine, even though it has never been used. Fantastic! It even sounds like it is perfectly legal. I ask Per what is needed for us to use the service, and how much it could cost. In my head, I think this will cost tens of thousands of dollars.

"First and foremost, is Firas employed by Lund University?" Per asks.

"Eh, yes, soon he is. We will arrange for an employment to be backdated," I say with a guilty voice.

"Okay good, because that's important. We can only use the security company for employees," Per informs me.

"Okay," I say. "How much do you think it might cost," I wonder worriedly.

"I'll find out. We procure this as a whole package. As a door-to-door service. A carrier should pick up Firas and his family in Iraq, and drive them to an appropriate airport. Then they fly with anonymous tickets to Sweden — well, it will be Denmark in this case, to Kastrup Airport, where they are picked up by car, which takes them to their home. The security company also ensures that the home is safe," says Per.

I'm totally amazed. I ask him why they should check if the home is safe. Yes, the family is Yazidi. No, you cannot tell if there is any threat to them in Sweden. I haven't thought about that.

Per says that the overall security picture is important, and Yazidi are a vulnerable group. As for the cost of the entire rescue action, it depends on how it will be done.

"We can fly them home all the way in a helicopter, if you want. But it will be very expensive," says Per, laughing now.

"If we use regular tourist-class air tickets, and a reasonably-priced carrier in Iraq, then it doesn't have to be that expensive. I will get back to you about that," Per says, and we end the conversation.

Everything Per has said buzzes in my head. It's amazing that there are solutions. I was prepared to come up with a new home-made solution, but now it may be arranged in a more organized way. Per is really a competent security manager, I think, when I realize that I was supposed to buy lunch. I'm really late to my lunch meeting with Jiayin. I hurry up along Sölvegatan towards the Thai wagon. Two other scientists I recognize from Chemistry stand before me in the queue. I greet them, but I don't start a conversation. I'm too stressed and out of focus right now. It's my turn, and I order rice with two different spicy dishes. One with curry and one with peanut sauce.

"Would that be all?" says the young lady from inside the caravan, or whatever you might call the vehicle from which the Thai food is served.

"Yes, please. Can I have a small cup with cashew nuts too?" I ask. I think this day will surely be long. It is always good to have some snacks in the office.

I pay with Swish, and hurry back to the Chemistry Center. Jiayin waits in the lunch room. She has already eaten her lunch. We sit and chat. I tell her about the whole situation with Firas. Just as I sit there and talk, I suddenly think that maybe I shouldn't talk so much about Firas's situation anyway. I think about what Per told me, that we have to take care of the entire security situation. Maybe Firas and his family are actually threatened here in Sweden too. Maybe there are ISIS supporters here who will contact them as soon as they get home. I should be more careful. Perhaps the radio interview was a stupid idea, although Firas was kept anonymous.

I bring a cup of coffee back to my office. I see on my computer screen that I have several new emails. One of them is from the department's personnel manager.

> Hi Lotta. Now there is a new employment decision for Firas as a PhD student in analytical chemistry. The employment decision is attached. I have also asked the payroll office to be quick on the payment of salary. Yours sincerely.

I respond directly with a big "THANK YOU" and I just feel a pure and wonderful joy. The employment proof shows that Firas was hired on the 1st of March earlier this year. My bosses including the dean are really prepared to think flexibly. I am delighted, and a sense of pride in my university is spreading in my chest.

I read and respond to more emails when my work phone suddenly rings. It's Per calling again. He says that he now has a good, really affordable proposal for a rescue operation. The entire operation will cost a few thousand dollars. What a great deal, I think. How is that even possible!

Per also says that to pursue this, he needs a lot of information about the family, their passports, where they are, if it is safe, etc. He carefully informs me about exactly what I should ask Firas, including if it is safe. But they are in the middle of a war zone. Obviously, the place is not safe, and that is exactly why they want to get out of there. I still understand what Per means — the transport company probably does not want to send a car into an area where there is full-scale war. Really, I have to check with Firas about this.

We end the call and I write a text message to Firas:

Hello, Firas. Are you OK today? I have talked to Per at the university security today. We can try to help you out from Iraq when you feel ready to leave with your wife and children. You decide when. We do need to get some questions answered though: 1. Your birth years (whole family); 2. Ability to move, like physical and mental capability; 3. Do you find your way around well in that area? 4. What is the situation like there now? Are there militaries around? What kind? (Kurds, ISIS, or what). Are the roads blocked by military? What happens in the area right now? 5. Do you all have your passports? What are your nationalities (whole family); 6. Can you drive a car in the area? Do you have access to a car? 7. Do you have food and water? For how much longer can you stay where you are now? I am sorry, these were many questions. Just do your best. Regards, Lotta.

It is a long, almost two hour wait, for Firas's answers. As always, I am worried about the waiting. Finally, a rather confusing text message comes, not really answering my questions:

> Dear Lotta. Today I will try to find an internet center. I took pictures of children and people living in schools. I will answer all your questions. Now I am busy with helping the others. You are my ideal. Regards, Firas.

I text him right away:

> OK, great! Be careful! How can you be sure ISIS will not enter Duhok and attack you?

Firas answers:

> I am not sure, but as I told you, in this moment we have no choice. Now there is a war between Kurdish militia and ISIS along the borders between Duhok and Mosul and we have no idea how long time the Kurdish militia can be standing.

I am really getting worried about this now. Firas is out helping people and taking pictures. He could be caught anytime soon. I text him back:

> So how can you say that you are safe?? You are not safe at all. Unless you can look into the future. If you answer questions 1-7 in the previous SMS I can prepare help for you. After that, it is up to you if you want the help. But it takes time to prepare these things! So please, just send an SMS with the answers. Thank you, Firas! Regards Lotta.

My text message was a bit harsh, but it worries me that Firas is not taking this (or me) as seriously as he should. Or did he give up already? Maybe he doesn't believe that I can actually help him? Firas's answer comes a bit later:

Oh Lotta. I am panicked but I am trying to calm down. Below are my answers.

Firas explains in the message that the whole family has their passports, that there is a war going on very nearby, that they do not have a car, but that they do have food and water. He has no idea for how long they can stay in the storage of the abandoned warehouse, it would depend on for how long time the Kurdish militia can be standing. Firas ends his message with:

I wish I can leave as soon as possible. Maybe I could rent a car and drive towards Turkey. Kind regards, Firas.

I am happy to see all the answers from Firas, and I hope that being very concrete and forward looking, he would understand that there is at least a small chance that we can get him out of Iraq. I forward his answers to Per, who immediately would like some clarifications. I send another SMS to Firas:

Follow up question: can you give a more detailed description on how the situation is in Duhok? Is the city safe to walk around in? Is it controlled by Kurds? Describe it as well as you can. Sorry for all these questions. How would you get to Turkey by car? Across the mountains? No militaries controlling? Regards, Lotta.

Firas and I continue writing many text messages back and forth about possibilities for Firas to travel across the mountains and to Turkey. I have just heard on the news how dangerous that is. People get killed. Finding a car, bus or taxi to get to Turkey the mountain-way should be plan B. Perhaps Firas is thinking that such route is plan A. He promised to find out more about which roads that are blocked and which ones are pretty much okay. The small dirt roads through the mountainous area are probably still open.

I spend the evening in my garden. After sunset, the sky is full of stars. Our neighbors have a barbecue party and seem to have a nice time. They drink wine and talk happily, a little louder than usual. Not at all annoying, just homely. Kuria and I talk about a little bit of everything. We talk about the next day when we will take Gabriel to the audiologist to examine his hearing. If he has very selective hearing, it is an important puzzle piece to a neuropsychiatric diagnosis. We believe Gabriel "just" has ADHD. Tomorrow is also the last day before I travel to a conference in Durban, South Africa. In my head, I think of everything I have to do tomorrow. In addition, I hope that Per has established a plan for how we can help Firas get home from the war in Iraq.

Silence spreads throughout the neighborhood. Even our wine-drinking neighbors have now moved into their house. All I can hear from outside is the gentle wind and the sound from a lonely common blackbird singing.

Chapter Ten

Firas's Story

Duhok, Iraq, 13th of August 2014

I sent the SMS that includes my answers to Lotta and found Maxim, who said he was bored of staying in this store for such a long time.

"When are we leaving from here?" Maxim asked.

"I don't quite know when, but soon!"

"When soon?"

"Maybe days or weeks, but we will leave here and return to Sweden."

I wasn't sure whether we could leave this place or not. Or I thought that maybe we will flee to another place, or maybe Lotta will save us or this attempt will also fail. But I had hope of leaving soon, so I was able to answer Maxim's question. But then I had a thought! What if I didn't receive a message from Lotta and there's no attempt from anyone to save us? What would I answer him then?

"I want a football! Can you buy one for me?"

"I'm so sorry, dear! I am afraid that I cannot right now! But when I go to the market to buy food, I'll buy one for you."

Maxim left bored and also disappointed. I was saddened to see him like this, and suddenly I had an idea. Although it was a ridiculous one, I was hoping it would bring some fun to Maxim. I took a cardboard and cut it by my hand into small pieces and then put it in a plastic bag. I filled the bag well until it became the size of football, then tightened the bag tightly and wrapped it with several other bags so as not to rupture quickly. Rawya came up to me and asked, "What are you doing?"

"I made a football for Maxim to play with. He is bored. He asked me to buy him a ball. I hope it will entertain him for today and tomorrow I will go to buy a real one."

"Such a good idea, although the shape of your ball is not completely spherical! Do you think it will roll?" Rawya said and in her words, there was a kind of encouragement mixed with irony.

I tightened the last plastic bag tightly and then I answered Rawya, "I don't know! We will try! Can you just go back a bit? I'll pass the ball to you."

Everyone was looking at us with astonishment. Rawya stood at a distance from me. I put the ball on the ground and then kicked it towards her. The ball rolled toward Rawya without deviating. She stopped the ball and then passed it towards me again. Maxim was sitting with the other children.

"Maxim!" Maxim turned to me, then I kicked the ball towards him.

Maxim got up and grabbed the ball with his hand and began to examine it with surprise:

"What is this?"

"It's a ball! You can play with it until I buy a real one."

Maxim put the ball on the ground and started kicking it and running behind it. The other children started running behind the ball as well and joined Maxim as they laughed. At that moment there was a joyful atmosphere and I saw the smile on my mother's face and the faces of the rest of the family as they were watching the children having fun.

***

Lotta's Story

Lund, Sweden, 13th of August 2014

Hello, Firas. We are trying from Lund to arrange with a safe taxi for you to get to an airport and then home. I will know more later. You cannot trust any taxi. It is better if we arrange with a company that has an agreement with Lund University. Regards, Lotta.

Oh, Lotta thanks a lot. I don't know what I have to say in this situation, but be sure that I will never ever forget what you are doing. You gave me a hope. Thank you. Regards, Firas.

Firas, there are still flights from Erbil for instance with Pegasus airlines. Can you get to Erbil (or is it Irbil?) I am not sure the safest way to travel there, if the road through Mosul is safe or the mountain road is better. On Friday we will pay your salary but it might take a few days before you see the money on the bank account. Are you sure you can get the money from the account from there? Or some kind of money-wiring is better? Regards, Lotta.

Dear Lotta. The road through Mosul is impossible but there is a safe road through the mountains. I found an ATM machine in a Kurdistan bank and they told me that I can make a withdrawal. I thought that there were no flights from Erbil. Many thanks. Regards, Firas.

After spending the morning in a waiting room at the hospital for my son's appointment with the audiology doctor, giving me a chance to send and read SMS between me and Firas, I return home to continue preparing for my trip. Once home in the kitchen, after dropping my son at school (and his hearing turned out to be perfect), I decided to call Firas. I tell him about the whole progress about the arrangement with his employment, the salary, the security company and other things going on in Lund. We just talk. It is so nice to hear his voice, and learn more about the life in Duhok for him and all the other Yazidis. This time, the phone line was not as good as it was previously, and it is not possible to hear well what Firas is saying. The sound keeps on going on and off all the time. Annoying. I decided to continue the conversation by SMS instead.

> Hello Firas. The reception was not good. Lund University will book the flight tickets for you! What day are you ready to leave??

> Dear Lotta, I am ready to travel any time and you can give them my phone number. I am happy to hear your voice and the happy news from you. Many thanks, you are a hero. Regards, Firas.

> I still do not know exactly when you will be picked up. There are flight tickets available for Monday. I will let you know. Regards, Lotta.

Things are about to work out. Soon the rescue operation can start; I can sense it. Per is giving me updates several times per day now. All my bosses have approved of this rescue. We have also decided that the cost for this rescue operation will be paid by Firas and his family. It will simply be drawn from his salary over the next several months. This is really doable since the cost is not that high. I am very grateful for that. Tax money should, of course, be used carefully, and at the university, this money should be used for core activities such as teaching and research. It should actually not be spent on bringing staff back home from weddings abroad. Although, I think that sometimes, one has to do the right thing. Sometimes, it is the right thing to do something that is formally wrong. This is just my personal thought, and in this case, we are lucky that the rescue operation is not an expensive affair. Firas can handle it with his salary as a doctoral student.

***

Lund, Sweden, 14th of August 2014

"Yes! Fantastic" I shout on the phone. Per has just told me that he has arranged the transport in Iraq. Two vehicles with drivers and armed men can go to Duhok any day to pick up Firas, his wife and two small children.

"Anonymous airline tickets are booked for the whole family from Erbil to Copenhagen, via Ankara and Istanbul. The flight leaves very early on Tuesday, and they land in Copenhagen the same day," Per says.

"So, they get picked up in Duhok on Monday...?" I wonder.

"Yes, that's right. If Firas and his family are ready then," Per responds.

"The children are three and six years old. Then they need car seats when picked up at the airport in Copenhagen," Per continues objectively.

"Ha-ha very funny. If the family manages to survive the ISIS war in Iraq and a return trip through the mountains of northern Iraq and beyond by plane, then maybe car seats for the kids are the least problem," I laugh to Per. Per does not laugh back.

"This is a door-to-door service, and the safety aspect also applies in Denmark and Sweden. The children must, of course, have car seats," says Per bitterly.

He is really professional, I think.

"OK. The three-year-old needs a real car seat for young children, but for the six-year-old it is enough with a booster seat," I say.

"Good, then I will notify the security company," says Per with authority.

"Perfect" I say and we end the conversation. Imagine, in only five days, the rescue operation will start for real!

In-between doing laundry and preparing for my trip to Durban, I send a text message to Firas:

Hello, Firas! Per has booked flight tickets for you on Tuesday at 03:20. Here is information about the company who will take you from Duhok to Erbil. They have your name and phone number also. You will not pay them anything, Lund University takes care of this. Alpafour Group is the name of the company. You should make arrangements with them. Per and Maggan will meet you at Kastrup airport. You will get someone to talk to about all that you have experienced, and this is something important for your mental health. Unfortunately, I am going for a conference in South Africa this afternoon. Otherwise I would have been the first one to give you a big hug at Kastrup! :) Take care and good luck now!! Call or SMS any time of the day. Best regards, Lotta.

I inform Firas about the names and phone number of all key people involved in the rescue operation.

Lotta, that is great! Thank you very much. I'll call the transport company. Warm regards Firas.

Very good. Bon voyage! Have a safe trip! :) Regards, Lotta.

I open Facebook and post a message for all my friends, especially for Hedvig:

Lund University is the best university in the world! Now they are going to arrange home transport of my doctoral student and his family from northern Iraq! :) As soon as he is home, I and others can tell more about this touching story. Right now, I just feel proud of my university!

In the afternoon I hug my family good bye, and I take the train across the Öresund bridge from southern Sweden to Denmark, to Kastrup airport. My flight to Durban is leaving at 18:30. In the airplane, I continue preparing for my lecture that I will give in a few days in the conference. I have the usual tray dinner. I picked chicken, and with that, a glass of white wine. I doze off, accompanied by a sunset over southern Europe somewhere.

***

Firas's Story

Duhok, Iraq, 14th of August 2014

ISIS fighters were still making progress towards Duhok and Erbil, where the terrorist organization managed to cut off the roads between them and occupied many cities and villages near Duhok and Erbil. Peshmerga forces reorganized and valiantly defended the Kurdistan region. However, ISIS fighters were less than 20 kilometers from where we were hiding. From time to time we heard explosions coming from the front lines of the battle, which was no longer far from us. At night, when there is still silence, we hear gunfire and explosions as a result of fighting between Peshmerga forces and ISIS fighters.

That day in the afternoon, when I was sitting with Rawya and my mother, I received a message from Lotta telling me that Per has booked flight tickets for me and my family on Tuesday at 3:20. Rawya noticed a smile on my face for the first time since I arrived in Iraq. I directly replied to Lotta, "Oh! Great thank you very much. I'll call the company. Warm regards, Firas"

"What's the matter?" Rawya asked eagerly.

"Wait a moment! I have to make a phone call first and then I will tell you."

I had told Rawya that I was in contact with Lotta and that she was worried about us, but I didn't tell her all the details, so I wouldn't give her false hope. When I sent my first SMS to Lotta I was desperate and helpless too. I just wanted to talk to someone outside of this zone of danger, filled with fear, terror, anxiety, news of death, and gunfire. I had no hope of returning to Sweden again to finish my studies. I had no hope of surviving or saving my family from death. And because I lost hope of getting out of this trap that I was stuck in with my family and returning to Sweden again. I was stuck in fear, horror, despair, and helplessness. I was in a state of extreme surrender after all my attempts to save my family failed.

I know Lotta well and I know how she treats her students and cares about them as if they are members of her family. But the matter was different at that time, in the university. I could not even imagine for a moment that she could save me from this predicament, but I even never thought that anyone could. Lotta has given me hope again and my perception has changed since I received her first message. It is the hope that showed me that in the sad tears of Rawya and my mother, there will be tears of joy shed when we survive. It is the hope that showed me in the frightened faces of Maxim and Enana, the smile of joy as they kicked the ball and ran after it on the lawns in Lund. And when the night came, and we locked the door of the store behind us, the darkness pervaded, and the atmosphere became suffocating from the heat. This hope opened a small window in the wall, emitting a light that expels the darkness, allowing a cool and refreshing air to soften this suffocating atmosphere. Day after day, this window was getting bigger and bigger.

I called the phone number that Lotta sent me, and someone with a hoarse voice replied, "Yeah! You are talking with X1!"

I didn't know whether it was his real name or a pseudonym, but I didn't care about this detail at that time.

"It is Firas. I am a Doctoral student from Lund University."

"Hi, Firas! I know that you are not in good condition, so I will not ask you about your conditions. Give me your address so we can come get you and your family."

I provided him with my address and described where we are hiding.

"Okay! We'll have you tomorrow. Let's be in constant touch."

"Okay!"

I closed the line and went to Rawya, who was watching me talk on the phone.

She asked again, "What is going on?"

I told Rawya what was happening and that Lotta had hired a security company to save us and that the mercenaries would come tomorrow to send us back to Sweden. Rawya rejoiced and hugged me as she cried. My mother and the rest of my family were listening to me while I told them what was going on, and they all rejoiced. Our lips have not formed a smile since before the ISIS attack, but the smile quickly disappeared from my face after I realized the bitter truth that I will not be able to take any of my family members. I will have to leave them behind me here in this place, facing their unknown fate.

Now it's real! With the help of Lund University, Lotta was able to complete all the procedures related to the rescue operation, such as an agreement with a security company, booking airline tickets and a plan to move us from this store in Duhok to Lund, Sweden. I was overwhelmed by a great feeling at that moment. A few days ago, I felt I had no value. But now I feel like I am king. I wrote a SMS and sent it to Lotta:

> Dear Lotta. I am sorry for bothering you, but what you did make me feel like a king. It is too much. Because of you, I feel safer and I feel that there are angels around me that protect my whole family. Many thanks for you and Lund University. Regards, Firas.

Then Lotta replied:

> Firas, if I did not believe in angels, I would not have named my son Gabriel! ;) People are more important than Chemistry. When we are all in Lund, we shall celebrate! And of course, you are a king! :) I am glad I could help. Regards, Lotta.

***

The Kocho massacre
Kocho, Iraq, 15ᵗʰ of August 2014

On 15 August 2014, while we were hiding in the warehouse and waiting in anticipation for what would happen to us in the coming days, ISIS was committing a massacre against unarmed civilians in a village called Kocho — a small village about 21 km from Sinjar district. ISIS had occupied it and besieged its inhabitants since the first day of Sinjar's fall. Kocho village has a population of about 1,700, all of them were Yazidis and only about 300 people managed to escape from the village a few hours earlier. Those who were able to escape went towards Mount Sinjar.

A few days before the massacre, the villagers received calls from the Sheikhs of Sunni Arab neighbors to assure them that they were safe and asked the villagers to stay in the village, asserting that they would not be harmed, but ISIS fighters erected barriers around the village, trapping residents inside.

ISIS fighters had given the villagers three days to either convert to Islam or to be killed. Despite the threat, the villagers refused to convert to Islam. The Mukhtar of the village said, "We were born in Iraq and have lived in it for thousands of years, and we respect Islam as well as the other religions."

The Mukhtar and the villagers called everyone they knew and anyone who had authority in the Iraqi government and the Kurdistan Regional Government (KRG) to rescue them, but there was no one to help. Both the Iraqi government and the KRG were in a state of constant retreat and disarray, making the villagers easy prey for terrorists.

At 9:30 am on August 15, 2014, a truck carrying large numbers of terrorists entered the village. They then gathered all the villagers — men, women, children and old people — in the village school, where they put the women and children, who numbered more than 800 women and children on the top floor, and about 400 men on the ground floor, and told them that they would take them to the city of Mosul. ISIS fighters told the residents not to be afraid and to bring with them all the things that they could carry, especially money, gold, and other valuables.

All the villagers were gathered in the school, which was surrounded by many ISIS terrorist fighters. An Islamic state commander, in a threatening form, asked the villagers to convert to Islam and told them that it was their last chance to survive.

The Mukhtar of the village, who was later killed, said, "How can I convince a 70-year-old to change his religion in just three days? We are our religion and you are your religion."

The villagers were then asked to hand over their money and valuables in preparation for relocation to Mosul, all while threatening to kill everyone that hid a phone or money. ISIS fighters brought cars and told the men that they would take them from the village to Mosul as a first stage, and then bring their women and children. The men rode in cars that were surrounded by heavily armed ISIS fighters. The cars drove off, but they took a road contrary to what was agreed upon. The men then realized that it was a hoax and that ISIS fighters would execute them. Several men tried to escape but were shot and executed immediately.

ISIS fighters landed the men in different places outside the village and ordered them to lie on their stomachs. There were about 400 men and young men. Then ISIS operatives began shouting "Allahu Akbar ... Allahu Akbar" and they shot the men and executed them all; only one man managed to survive. Women and children were transferred to Mosul to be distributed to ISIS fighters as spoils of war.

***

Lotta's Story

Durban, South Africa, 15th of August 2014

I landed on the King Shaka international airport just north of Durban in the mid-day. The air feels cooler and more humid than in Sweden now. Durban is located on the coast of the Indian Ocean. I wonder if people swim in the sea here, if there are nice sandy beaches. This is my first time in Durban. I sit and relax in the taxi on my way to the hotel,

Southern Sun Elangeni & Maharani. Sky-scrapers border the highway through the city. Everything looks very big, and I have a hard time deciding if I'm close to the city center or not. Soon we arrive at my hotel, which is just a stone's throw from a long, beautiful sandy beach. I check into my room and unpack my clothes and few other things. I have a fantastic view from my window that extends from floor to ceiling and from wall to wall. I throw myself on the bed and look up at the ceiling. I just need some rest. Before I fall asleep, I log into the hotel's network to check if I have any missed messages. No, not a single one. I send a text message to Kuria:

> "Hi, Kuria. I just landed in Durban, and the trip went well! The weather is much like home. The beach is close. Give the guys a hug! Love, Lotta"

I also send a text message to Firas:

> "Firas. Are you OK today? Just checking on you… ;)"

Amazingly, Firas answers right away, just as if he was sitting there holding the phone, waiting for a message:

> "Dear Lotta, I am fine and happy that I will leave soon. Many thanks. Regards, Firas."

> "Great! :) Take it easy and avoid taking pictures, just in case. Regards, Lotta"

***

After resting for a few hours in my room, I decided to find something to eat, and to take a walk along the beach. I learned that the security level in Durban around this and other expensive hotels is very high. Guards stop you if you walk too far away from the beach, or if you get the crazy idea of wanting to walk inland, towards downtown. That is simply not allowed. The security cannot be guaranteed. After enjoying a huge seafood salad and a walk to the end of the permitted part of the beach and back, I returned to my room in the hotel and checked out the conference program. I noticed that it will start with registration and a welcome reception Sunday in the late afternoon. That means that I have one and a half days to enjoy Durban. Perhaps I can go for a tour of downtown with other tourists here at the hotel. At the very least, I would like to bring home some aromatic spices like curries with me.

Late in the evening, while I was getting ready for bed in my hotel room, I hear a beep from my cell phone. It is a text message from Firas.

Dear Lotta, a few days ago I was desperate and I had three main problems. — Neither me nor my whole family feel safe and we are living in this storage — I have no money to bring my wife and children to home (Sweden) — Even if I manage to be in Sweden, I have no money to pay the rent, buy food and complete my PhD study because I have no idea when the Kurdistan ministry of Science will pay my salary and tuition fee. I was looking at the boxes in this storage and felt that these boxes are more important than me, believe me, I felt that I am equal to nothing and no one cares about me nor to my family in this dirty place. Then you came like a light through the darkness, enlightening my road and giving me hope. You managed to solve all these problems, bring back my family to home and save my PhD studies. And because of you, I can send money to my family to buy food and survive. Because of you, all of us feel safe and protected. Many thanks to you, my angel. Bless you. Bless your kids. Bless your husband. Bless Sweden. Kind regards, Firas.

As I read the message, tears begin to flow down my cheek. I don't notice it first. It's so sad, this whole story. Such hopelessness Firas must feel. The whole family trusts that he will arrange everything, but he is stuck in a life-threatening situation. What despair he must feel. Yet it is his country and his compatriots who are his traitors. I sense a pain in my chest. I find it amazing that he can feel such happiness over the little things I have done. It's nothing. Some phone calls, some emails, some fixing and trixing. Not much at all. But honestly, I'm afraid now. I am afraid that ISIS will soon march into Duhok and capture all women and children, and execute all the men. I see this in front of me as I read Firas's message. May our help arrive on time! There are only two things that matter now; that Firas and his family come home in one piece from the war in Iraq, and that Firas may complete his doctoral studies in Lund and become a doctor in analytical chemistry! I write back to Firas before I switch off the bed light in my hotel room in Durban:

> Thank you, Firas! You are too kind!! If I had known that you had no money, I would have solved this sooner! I was raised in a democratic home and my parents were always kind to people. I also protect equal opportunity. Why should anyone prevent you from getting your PhD? I will not be relaxed until you are home with your family and then when I am also home, we will celebrate! We also need to make sure that you get the help you need after this trauma. Warm regards, Lotta.

***

Durban, South Africa, 18th of August

It's been three days since I arrived in Durban. I have tried to relax, toured a bit in Durban, visited a museum, bought spices, and walked along the beach every day. The conference started yesterday afternoon. I met a lot of researchers I've met already before. Researchers from South Africa, various European countries, and from the USA. Even some researchers from Asia, including South Korea, Japan, and China. Our big common interest is green chemistry. This means chemistry that enables the production and use of chemicals in a better way for the environment than has previously been the case. Tomorrow, I will present my own research on how to use supercritical carbon dioxide as a solvent instead of using ether, toluene, or chlorinated solvents.

Carbon dioxide is an environmentally friendly solvent, at least if it can be reused many times in the processes.

Right now, I sit and drink coffee and eat a fantastic, great tasting breakfast omelet in the hotel restaurant. If there's something I appreciate, it's the breakfast buffet, at least in hotels where they can make a good omelet.

"Would you like some more coffee?" asks the polite waiter.

"Oh, yes thanks, with milk," I answer him.

There is still an hour left until the conference begins. I have time to sit for a while at the breakfast table. I see several conference delegates with name tags hanging around their necks. Everyone has the same green colored laces to hold their name tags.

"Here you go, some coffee, ma'am," says the waiter.

"Thank you so much," I tell him.

Suddenly I realize that today is the big day for Firas! Today he and his family will be picked up! May it go well! I send him a SMS:

Firas, today is the big day! I hope everything goes well!!!

Good morning Lotta! I feel like I am in one of the Hollywood movies!!! Of course, you are playing the biggest role in this movie! Everything is fine. Regards, Firas.

Thank you Firas! You have to play well today! ;) Remember to send a SMS to Per in Lund so that he can follow your traveling. Cheers Lotta.

I am in constant contact with my friend the journalist, Hedvig, as well as with Swedish radio journalists in national radio. There is one journalist for the Swedish radio who would like to speak to Firas again, when he is in a safe place, far away from ISIS troops. I text Firas again:

> Firas, let me know when you are in a safe place in Erbil. Also, a journalist, the same you talked to last time, wants to call you later today. It is alright as long as you do not give her your name. You are becoming a media person! ;) Cheers, Lotta.

Chapter Eleven

Firas's Story

Duhok, Iraq, 18th of August 2014

On Monday, August 18, at 11:30 am, while exchanging encouraging text messages with Lotta, I received a phone call from X1. He was telling me that they were in Duhok and that they were on their way to the storage facility. I had nothing to take with me but the fear, anxiety, and pain that I would feel as I left, leaving my mother and my family in this wretched place. We only had my little bag in which I put some water and food in preparation for our journey into the unknown. We didn't know if it would succeed this time or fail like our previous attempts. The road to Erbil was long and dangerous and we were still trapped in Duhok.

I told Rawya when the car was supposed to arrive. I then spoke with my brothers and asked them to take care of the family in my absence. We all hugged each other and cried. I kissed the nieces and nephews, as well as my mother and all my sisters and brothers-in-law, as if to say goodbye to them, thinking I might never see them again.

I sat on the ground with Rawya beside me, and my mother, my siblings, and their children all gathered around us. I looked at their faces, all tired and filled with fear, and I was overcome with the notion that I could not leave them under these circumstances and that I had to give up this idea of trying to escape. I told my mother:

"I won't go and leave you here. I'll stay with you and we will either face death together or survive together."

"Yes! Yes! We won't leave! We'll stay here too," Rawya agreed, crying profusely.

"No, my son! Don't do it! You must leave this place, not just for you and your family, but for all of us. Even if something bad happens to us, I'll be reassured that you and your children are fine and that you will remember us," my mother said, with tears streaming down her cheeks. Then she grabbed Rawya by the hand and said to her, "You have to leave now, my daughter, and take care of Maxim and Enana. You must leave and save yourselves."

Rawya was very sad because she could not see her family before our departure as they were staying in another shelter, some distance from the storage facility where we were hiding. Because the situation was very dangerous, and the possibility of our movement was very limited, Rawya called her parents and siblings to tell them about Lotta and the security company, and to say goodbye to them through her tears.

All we could do now was to sit in the storage facility, waiting for the security company to come to save us. Everyone was sad, and Rawya, my mother, and my sisters did not stop crying. At approximately 12 noon, my phone rang. It was X1.

"We're close to the place you described to us."

"Okay! I'll be outside of the building waiting for you."

My family and I exited the storage facility and waited for the car to come. I was startled to see two white SUVs rapidly approaching. We all panicked, fearing that they were not from the security company, but that the two cars belonged to Islamic extremist groups. We retreated and I pulled Maxim and Enana toward me, as Rawya clung to my arm. The two SUVs sped straight toward us along the unpaved dirt road leading to the storage, leaving a cloud of dust behind them. Then they came to an abrupt halt directly in front of us. The dust storm kicked up by the two SUVs created very poor visibility. Four armed men, dressed in military-style clothing, led by a dark-skinned man, emerged from the dust cloud. He came toward us and when his eyes fell upon me, he approached and said:

"It's good to see you safe. X1 has come to take you to a safer place."

I turned to my mother and hugged her, as did Rawya, and we bid farewell to our family. We were all crying, but X1 shouted with a firm voice.

"We have to hurry. Our journey is long, we must reach Erbil before dark."

We headed toward the two SUVs, whose engines were still running, and there was a driver sitting in each vehicle. The commandos equipped us all with bullet-proof vests and helmets, and then Rawya and I, along with the children, climbed in the back of one of the vehicles, while X1 rode with us in the front seat, placing his weapon on his lap, in a state of readiness, while the other three commandos rode in the second SUV.

As soon as we closed the doors of the vehicle, we sped on our way to Erbil. Rawya and I turned to look at our families as a last farewell, but in a few seconds, they disappeared in the dust raised by the speeding vehicles.

***

X1 ordered the commandos in the other SUV to stay in front of us, and to remain alert, to monitor the road carefully, and to be prepared for any emergency. The SUVs did not take the usual road between Erbil and Duhok because it was closed. They also avoided the checkpoints packed with people. Instead, they took another route I had never seen before. The road was fairly flat with a number of hills and highlands on either side, but what caught my attention, after driving for over an hour, was that the road was completely desolate of both cars and people.

We had traveled quite some distance from Duhok, and I looked around to figure out our location, but I couldn't tell where we were or in which direction we were headed. Although the road was bumpy and long, running through the mountains, I felt kind of reassured. These mountains and the places we passed through were far away from where terrorists were. It was closer to the Iraqi-Iranian border. but I still feared the presence of bandits or groups loyal to ISIS, especially since the Kurdistan region was at war and there may also be sleeper cells here waiting for the right opportunity to announce a coup against the Kurdish government. The number of displaced people who had entered Kurdistan in the past few days exceeded one million and there were likely to be ISIS fighters among them.

After more than three hours driving along this narrow road running through the mountains, we received another call from the second SUV driving in front of us:

"X2 to X1, come in please."

"X1 to X2, I read you."

"We see a checkpoint in front of us."

"Can you identify them and how many are there?" X1 asked.

"They appear to be Kurdish forces and there doesn't seem to be more than six soldiers."

"It's unlikely for terrorists to be in this place. Nor can we go back, and there is no way to circumvent or to avoid them. Drive slowly and be prepared for any contingency. We will maintain a distance between us and you. Be quiet and tell them the truth and that we are on a security mission that requires the transfer of a family from Duhok to Erbil," X1 said.

"Roger."

Maxim and Enana had fallen asleep from fatigue, but Rawya and I remained vigilant, watching with concern. The second car arrived at the checkpoint and stopped, but we were driving slowly, with quite some distance behind them. The transmitter on their walkie talkie was left open, so we could hear what was transpiring between them and the soldiers at the checkpoint. The driver in the second car was a Kurd, so he took charge of talking to them. Although I am not fluent in Kurdish, I could understand a few words.

"Where are you coming from?" asked one of the soldiers at the checkpoint.

"We are coming from Duhok."

"And where are you going?"

"We are going to Erbil."

"Why are you carrying weapons and why are you taking this route?"

"We're on a security mission."

"I want to see your permits to carry the weapons and your IDs."

When I heard them ask for ID cards, I was frightened because I remembered what happened to the textile workers in Mosul and how they were killed based on their IDs. Now we also arrived at the checkpoint and stopped just behind the other SUV. Another soldier approached our vehicle. Before he arrived, X1 shut down the radio and we no longer knew what was going on between the soldiers and the other vehicle.

"Are you with the commandos in that vehicle?" The soldier asked, as he pointed his hand in the direction of the SUV parked in front of us.

"Yes!" The driver, who also seemed to be fluent in Kurdish, replied.

"Is it true that you are on a security mission?"

"Yes!"

The gunman looked at us, and, in the meantime, Maxim woke up and began to turn right and left afraid. Rawya put her hand on Maxim's shoulder and at the same time I put my hand on his head trying to reassure him.

"I want to see your IDs!" the soldier commanded us.

We didn't have our ID cards with us. In fact, since that fateful day, when the Yazidi workers had been killed in Mosul, I hadn't carried my ID, but I gave him our passports instead. The gunman looked at the passports and then at our faces. After checking the passports, he returned them back to us and then turned to his colleagues and advised them to allow us to cross. Once again, I felt relief. Then I looked at Rawya and saw her smiling at Maxim.

The journey took more than eight hours. We came across other checkpoints and by nightfall we finally arrived in Erbil. The situation in Erbil was extremely tense and the scenes on the streets were no different from those that we had witnessed in Duhok. We stopped at a hotel and X1 told us, "You will stay at this hotel tonight and at 02:00 am we will take you to Erbil airport."

"Will you leave us alone in the hotel?" Rawya asked with fear.

X1 turned to Rawya, smiled, and said, "Of course not! We will be here to protect you and we will not leave you until you enter the Erbil airport and your plane takes off and you are safely in the sky. Only then, our mission will be over."

"Thank you!" Rawya and I both replied.

Maxim woke up when we arrived, but Enana was still sleeping, so I carried her on my shoulder. Maxim grabbed his mother's hand and entered the hotel. We took the room keys from the reception and made our way to our room. We were all exhausted. I put Enana on the bed and then inspected the room. It was the first time in more than 12 days

that we had seen a bed. I threw myself on it, extremely fa-
tigued, while Maxim asked Rawya to turn on the TV. Rawya
turned on the TV and started browsing the channels in
search of something for the children. Most of the news channels were reporting on the events in Iraq, in particular the
murder and enslavement of Yazidis. She stopped searching
whenever she found a channel talking about the battles between Iraqi forces and Peshmerga on the one hand, and the
ISIS terrorists on the other. Maxim kept asking her to change
the channel and to continue to search for a children's cartoon
channel. Rawya and I were eager to hear the news on television. Since Rawya and the children escaped from Bashiqa
and I joined them in Duhok, we hadn't watched any television and the only news we received was by telephone.
Maxim shouted when he saw a children's program and
asked his mother not to change the channel this time. Maxim
then sat in front of the television watching the children's
programs, while Rawya sat on a chair in the room, contact-
ing her family and informing them of our arrival. I called my
mother as well and told her that we had arrived safely in
Erbil and they were all happy to hear this news. Then I sent
an SMS to Lotta:

> I'm in Erbil now. We're in the hotel and we're ok! Thank
> you! Regards, Firas.

***

Erbil, Iraq, 19th of August 2014

At 01:30 am, Rawya and I woke up to the sound of the alarm. After 10 minutes, X1 called.

"Good morning!" X1 said.

"Good morning!" I replied.

"Are you ready?"

"Yes!"

We only had a small bag, so it didn't take much time to prepare. The children were asleep. I carried Maxim and Rawya carried Enana and went out to find the two SUVs still outside waiting for us. Just like before, Rawya and I rode in the back of one SUV, together with the children, while X1 rode in the front seat, but this time we didn't wear bullet-proof vests and helmets. I also noticed that X1 wasn't carrying his machine gun or any other weapons. The other SUV drove in front of us and followed it to the airport. Before arriving at the airport, X1 spoke with the commandos in the other car and told them we would be departing shortly and told them not to go too far away.

"The airport is a security zone and we cannot enter it with weapons. So, I left my weapons in the other car," X1 explained.

The other SUV continued on its way as we turned toward the airport. After an inspection of us and our vehicle by airport security, we entered the airport. The SUV stopped in front of the passenger departure gate and X1 turned toward us and said, "You are now at the airport, which is a safe and protected area. But we will stay here until we make sure that you board the plane and you are on your way to Ankara. I want you to contact me immediately when you board a plane or if any emergency situation occurs."

"OK!" I answered.

"Have a safe trip."

"Thank you!"

"Good-bye!"

"Good-bye!"

We got out of the car and I carried Enana, who was still sleeping, on my shoulder. Rawya, Maxim and I walked toward the departure gate. Before passing through the gate, I stopped and turned to X1 and raised my hand to wave goodbye. Rawya also stopped and raised her hand. Maxim looked at us, and then looked at X1, and he waved his hand like us. X1 smiled at Maxim and waved his hand also.

***

We entered the airport and waited for the departure of our plane to Ankara International Airport in Turkey. After another inspection by airport security, we entered the waiting lounge. We sat there silently, feeling sad. We waited for a little over an hour, but it seemed like days.

During this waiting period, Rawya cried from time to time, and each time, Maxim kept asking her not to cry and he wiped her tears with his hands. Rawya stopped crying for a short time, but only for a few minutes, and then she would start again. I couldn't cry. I wanted to cry, but I couldn't. I had a heavy heart, anxiety, fear, and anger about what was happening to us. Enana was sitting in my lap and I was trying to play with her because she was only a four-year-old girl and I didn't want her to be affected by what was happening, especially because she wasn't fully aware of what was going on around us. But Maxim seemed to be aware of what was happening. He knew that we were running away from 'bad guys,' as he called them, and that these 'bad guys' wanted to kill us. The words 'kill us' seemed like such harsh words for a small child of Maxim's age. But what he couldn't understand was why they were pursuing us and wanted to kill us? A few days before, when we were still hiding in the storage facility, I sat looking at Rawya and my mother while they prepared what they could find for lunch. Maxim came and sat beside me, leaning his back against the wall, clamping his arms around his legs, and looking forward. After a short silence, he asked me, without looking at me:

"Have we made a mistake?"

I was shocked at this question. I looked at his face and I saw the fear in his eyes.

"I don't know what you mean, but we all make mistakes in our lives. These mistakes may be large or small, but the important thing is to learn from your mistakes and to try not to repeat them," I said, looking into his eyes.

"What mistake have we made to be chased by the bad guys who want to kill us?"

I realized from the way that he sat, his silence, and his steady look forward, that this question was not born of this moment, but rather one that he had on his mind for a long time. His question was the natural consequence of what he heard every day in the news, the stories of the horrific murders of Yazidis by the terrorists, and of the fear that he saw in the face of his mother and others as they fled from one place to another to escape death. He felt death was close to him and he began to realize its meaning, even though he was still only a six-year-old boy. His young mind interpreted death as a punishment for anyone who commits a sin. But he struggled to understand what mistake we had made to deserve this punishment, death. I put my hand on his head gently and asked him to look at me. Then I calmly replied:

"No, my son! We didn't make any mistakes for us to deserve what is happening to us. But you must know that this world is not a perfect place. It is filled with good and evil. As for these bad guys, they can be present at any time and any place. They want to kill us to seize our land and property. Good will triumph over evil in the end, just as it does in movies." Then I smiled at him and held him to my chest to make him feel safe.

It was difficult to explain to him the real reason why ISIS fighters pursued Yazidis and those of other religions to exterminate them. The answer to his question was very difficult. Even as adults, we are still unable to understand why this terrorist group has killed Yazidis with such brutality, enslaved women and children, and pursued others to exterminate them. How can the fact that we have a different religion be reason enough to kill us? How have these terrorists been persuaded that they are following God's orders to kill us and that doing so will bring them closer to Paradise? How can all these brutal acts of murder, rape, and enslavement please God? Where is the hand of God in all these acts? Is this really His wish and His will?

***

The airport was almost empty, except for a small number of passengers — no more than 200. Most airlines had suspended flights to Iraq for security reasons, and it seems that only our plane, and perhaps one other plane, would take off from Erbil airport today. I looked at the faces of other passengers who all seemed as fearful and tired as us. We were still in Erbil on the ground. Many things could still happen to stop our flight. One possibility was that our flight would be canceled like many other flights were canceled only hours before take-off. Another possibility was that if

ISIS terrorists advanced closer to the airport, the plane would be within the range of their missiles. The most catastrophic possibility was if ISIS stormed Erbil and seized the airport before our plane took off.

At 3:30 am, the plane moved on to the runway to take off. Rawya and Enana sat on one side of the aircraft, while Maxim and I sat on the other side across from them. Rawya leaned her head against the edge of the window and looked out at the runway. She was very sad and tears flowed down her cheeks. When the plane took off, Maxim held my hand firmly. He was afraid. I looked at him and smiled. "Don't be afraid, my dear boy! We're going home!"

Chapter Twelve

Firas's Story

From Erbil to Copenhagen, 19ᵗʰ of August 2014

Several hours later, our plane landed at Ankara International Airport. The only thing I remember upon our arrival in Ankara was that I sent a text message to Per informing him that we had landed. My mind was so clouded, I had little awareness of what was going on around me. I felt as if someone had hit me in the back of the head with a baseball bat. It was almost as if I was deaf, I don't remember hearing the sounds of the other passengers in the airport. I had mixed feelings; a sense of security and insecurity at the same time. I felt safe because I had arrived in Turkey and gotten Rawya, Enana, and Maxim out of danger, away from fear and terror, away from ISIS terrorists, and away from death. Despite this, the feeling of insecurity never left me. I was overwhelmed by fear and anxiety for my mother and my brothers, who I had left in that warehouse, filled with fear and horror, and surrounded by death that might strike at any moment. It was as if my body was on fire and then suddenly cold water was poured over me. I remember walking with fast and steady steps, carrying Enana on my shoulder and holding Maxim's hand with my other hand, while Rawya held Maxim's other hand. We held each other's hands intensely, afraid to be separated again. Although I was confused, I knew my destination — the gate with the flight to take us to Istanbul. The airport was crowded with passengers, and when I made my way there, I remembered the first day I arrived in Duhok and how I fought my way through the crowds to reach my family. But the difference here was that the throngs of passengers knew their destination and their faces were free from fear and anxiety, and I could see the smile on many of their faces. Unlike the crowds that I met in Duhok, which seemed like most of them were heading into the unknown, fear and anxiety had worn their faces. Those faces will remain stuck in my memory forever.

After the layover of less than two hours in Ankara, the plane took off for Istanbul. When we arrived at Istanbul airport, Rawya and the children collapsed from fatigue. They all slept on the airport benches. I sent a letter to Per informing him of our arrival in Istanbul. Our flight to Copenhagen was delayed by more than an hour for technical reasons. Finally, we were ready to take off and we were on our way to Copenhagen.

***

On the plane, Rawya sat next to Enana across the aisle from myself and Maxim. We sat silently, thinking about what happened to us and what would happen to our families and the Yazidis in Iraq. After more than an hour of flying, both Maxim and Enana felt bored. Enana looked at Maxim and gestured with her hand for him to come and sit next to her to play. Maxim smiled and got up from his seat and asked Rawya if he could sit in her seat next to Enana. They changed places. Rawya came and sat next to me and I grabbed her hand gently, then we both looked at the children. They talked and drew on paper they had obtained from the flight crew.

Rawya put her head on my shoulder and said, sadly, "Thousands of families are still stranded on Sinjar Mountain under very harsh conditions."

"They escaped death at the hands of ISIS terrorists to face another death. Death from hunger, thirst, and the hot sun," I added.

"Even the aid that is dropped to them from the planes does not reach them. It either falls too far from them on that rugged mountain or is damaged when it falls on the slopes of the mountain and hits the hard rocks," Rawya said.

"The process of evacuating people from the mountain is going slowly," I commented, "and with great caution, as the number of displaced people is in the tens of thousands."

"Why they don't send more helicopters to rescue them?" Rawya asked.

"It isn't easy. The mountain is surrounded by ISIS fighters, and helicopters must fly over the territory occupied by ISIS to reach Mount Sinjar. That is a dangerous process in it of itself."

We sat quietly for a while and then I added, "What tragic stories are told by the evacuees from Mount Sinjar. Many of them died of thirst and extreme heat. Also, the lack of food has caused many deaths, as they were forced to eat tree leaves and inedible plants."

"Aren't there any water springs on the mountain?" Rawya asked.

"Yes, there are, but ISIS intentionally bombs the area around them with mortar shells and sets up ambushes to capture those who come near the springs to get a little water."

"How do the ISIS terrorists know the whereabouts of these springs?" Rawya asked.

"Many of the ISIS fighters are residents of the Arab villages surrounding Sinjar and have participated in the killing of men, captivity of women and children, and the looting of Yazid property and property," I explained. "They were not satisfied with this, so they revealed to ISIS the locations of these springs, as well as the roads leading to the mountain and the caves that the people fleeing could take refuge in, as well as other routes that the displaced people might take to escape from Sinjar mountain, which has aggravated their suffering."

"What criminals!" Rawya exclaimed. She grew silent for a moment before she said, through her tears, "I felt a lot of pain in my heart when I heard the story of a Yazidi woman who rejoiced when she learned that she was pregnant after a long wait, but she did not expect her birth to be tragic. Days before she gave birth, she fled to the mountain and she went into labor in a cave. But she suffered severe bleeding during childbirth, which led to her death. Her baby died a few hours later."

Tears also poured out of my eyes. I wiped my tears and then turned to Maxim and Enana, who were busy drawing and talking to each other.

***

Lotta's Story

Durban, South Africa, 19th of August 2014

In the morning, I went to the conference hall to give my keynote lecture. I'm not the least bit nervous. This is nothing compared to fleeing away from ISIS. I'm just doing my job. I give my talk, I discuss and I answer questions, and I listen to other lectures. A very ordinary day at work, actually.

I was feeling so relieved after receiving that message from Firas saying that he and his family arrived safely in Erbil. I strongly sensed that this rescue operation would work out! Firas and his family will come back to Sweden! We will win! Science vs. ISIS, 1-0! In the evening, I celebrated with a glass of white wine — step 1 in this mission was complete! And this was the most crucial step. I wish I had someone to celebrate with, but I cannot tell anyone what is going on. Anyone who sees me, though, can see the smile on my face.

My lecture went really well, and while I having my afternoon coffee, I receive an email from Per. Of course, I check my emails every ten minutes or so.

> Hello. Firas and his family is currently in Ankara. Now a flight to Istanbul remains for further destinations Kastrup and Lund. Sincerely, Per G.

I answer him back:

> Excellent! Thank you! Regards, Lotta.

I attend the conference all through the afternoon, but I am having enormous difficulty focusing on the science. I check my emails regularly. Finally, I receive another email from Per.

> Hello again. Firas with family now came out of the Arrivals Hall at Kastrup (but without luggage) and are now on their way to Lund. Sincerely, Per G.

I respond immediately:

> Hello Per! Absolutely fantastic! Mission completed! :) Thank you for a tremendously professionally managed work! I will invite you for a coffee one day soon! Sincerely, Lotta.

I can breathe out. I know Maggan has received Firas with wife and children. This story has a happy ending. Again, I enter Facebook and post a message, this time for the whole world:

> Finally, my doctoral student is rescued from northern Iraq! It's a relief! Thanks to fantastic Lund University! There is an enormous competence to help in the right way when it really matters! Of course, my joy is split, given all the poor people who remain in northern Iraq, including my doctoral student's entire extended family.

***

Firas's Story

Copenhagen to Lund, Sweden, 19th of August, 2014

When our plane landed in Copenhagen, we exited the airport to find Per and Maggan waiting for us. They had come with an eight-passenger SUV and a driver to take us from the airport to our home in Lund. We hugged each other. Rawya was crying, and Maggan was very sad, while I still suffered from trauma.

"It's good to see you safe. Your plane was delayed for more than an hour coming from Istanbul," Per said, as he had been tracking the entire rescue operation from start to finish.

"Thank you very much! I don't know what to say," I replied, exhausted with fatigue.

"You don't have to say anything. You're all safe now."

Maggan hugged Rawya and told her, "Don't cry and don't be afraid. It's over and you're safe now."

"Maggan and the driver will take you to your home in Lund," Per told us. "I wish you a safe journey." He hugged each of us and said goodbye.

I rode in the back seat, Rawya, with Enana and Maxim sat in the seat in front of me, while Maggan rode in the front seat. The driver then drove towards Lund via the Öresund Bridge. As we crossed the bridge, I thought back to four years earlier when I crossed this bridge for the first time with Maxim and Rawya, who was then pregnant with Enana. I had hoped to finish my studies and go back to my country, but now, with the terrorists controlling our cities, there was little or no hope of ever returning.

As the SUV drove through the streets on the way to Lund, I looked through the window of the car to see people roaming the streets freely and safely, joyfully dressed in their beautiful summer clothes. The summer is such a wonderful and beautiful time in Sweden. Children walked in front of their parents with joy; some of them carrying balloons, while others ate ice cream. I could see families and elderly people sitting at tables outside cafes, restaurants, and bars, eating and drinking cold beer, talking happily. Then I asked myself, "Why? Why can't people in my country live and enjoy such peace and security?" I wished to see my mother, my siblings and their children walking around like these people, enjoying peace and feeling secure, instead of living in constant fear and sadness.

***

When we arrived in Lund, the driver stopped the SUV some distance from our apartment. He then got out of the vehicle and walked towards our house. Rawya turned to me, as surprised as I was, and asked, "We made it home. Should we get out here or what?"

Before I could answer, Maggan turned to us and said, "Don't be alarmed! He's not just a driver, he's a bodyguard and he has gone to check your apartment to make certain that it is safe."

I couldn't help myself any longer, tears began to stream down my cheeks and Rawya also began to cry. Maxim and Enana looked at us and they also started to cry. Maxim asked his mother, "Why are you crying?"

"Nothing, son! We are back home!"

"Don't cry, please!" Maggan said sadly.

Moments later, the bodyguard returned and reported that our apartment was safe. Then, he took us home and he left. Together with Maggan, we all entered our apartment. Maxim and Enana went straight to their room, pulled out their toys, and started playing with them as if they missed them a lot. As for me, Rawya and Maggan, we sat in the living room. We sat silently for a short time, then Rawya broke out in tears once more.

"No, my dear Rawya! You're safe now! Don't be afraid and don't worry!" Maggan said.

"Yes! We're safe, but what about the rest of our family in Iraq?" she replied as she continued to sob.

"It was a terrible experience for us, but our families are still living that nightmare," I said, putting my head in my hands.

Overwhelmed with sadness, Maggan asked, "Tell me how I can help you?"

"Dear Maggan! You all helped us so much! I didn't expect that at all. I thank you all from the bottom of my heart," I said

"We didn't do anything worthy of thanks. It's only human to help each other in time of need. I wish we could've rescued the rest of your family," Maggan said.

After a little more silence, Maggan added, "You're all exhausted. I'll leave you to rest. Do you have food in the house? Let me go to buy you some food."

"Thank you, dear Maggan, but you don't have to do that! You have done so much for us already," I answered.

"Thank you, Maggan! Thank you so much!" Rawya said, as she got up and hugged her.

"I'm very happy to see you safe again," Maggan said, still hugging Rawya.

After Maggan left, we stayed at home alone. I sat on the couch next to Rawya and embraced her.

"I hope that no harm will come to them! I hope someone will come to save them, just as we have been saved," Rawya said.

"I hope so too!" I answered, trying to hide my concern and doubt.

***

Lotta's Story

Durban, South Africa, 20th of August 2014

I am a practical and pragmatic person. Now Firas and his family are safe in Lund, but the question now is how do they really feel after what they have experienced? I search Google for information about post-traumatic stress. Apparently, there is a center in Malmö, just 15 km south of Lund, which takes care of people who suffer from this. I find a lot of information that I send to Firas via email:

> Hello, Firas. I have google-translated information about post-traumatic stress disorder and what help you can get, both for you, your wife and children. Maybe not perfectly translated, but better than nothing. Regards, Lotta.

The documents are called "Trauma and war experiences adults" and "Trauma and war experiences children," and I really hope that Firas seeks the help he should get, and that the whole family gets to talk to someone professional.

It's time for me to go back to Sweden and Lund. It is wonderful to come home, and the sooner I can meet Firas again, the better. I want to see how he's doing after all of this. Firas will be home resting for a few days before I contact him at all. I guess he and his family need some time to get settled and come to terms with the fact that they are home in Lund again. Again, I doze in an airplane watching a sunset, this time over Africa somewhere.

Chapter Thirteen

Days have passed since we had returned to Sweden. I used to find it very difficult to sleep as I had insomnia and could not fall asleep until very late hours. It was the same case was with Rawya. One night, at around two in the morning, I was smoking a cigarette in the balcony. The sky was clear, and although it was summer, the weather at these hours of the night is usually somewhat cold. I heard Rawya crying in her sleep, then she woke up scared, her breathing rushed. She looked around and didn't find me in the bed, then she called me, "Firas!"

"I'm here on the balcony," I replied.

It was another nightmare, the same that she used to have every night. It was almost the same nightmare that I had when I slept, and I feared that if I closed my eyes, I would see them. Despite our sense of safety, the fear and anxiety for our families still accompanied us. We were still in a state of shock and didn't believe that we were able to survive.

Rawya got up from the bed and went to the kitchen to drink water. She came to the balcony and stood next to me, then she said, "You are here again. You are smoking a lot and sleeping a little. Didn't you quit smoking? Why did you go back to it again?"

"I will stop smoking again! It seems that you had a nightmare again?"

"Yes! It is terrifying! Every day we hear dozens of horrific stories about the horrific crimes committed by radical Islamists against the Yazidis. And when I close my eyes, I imagine all these crimes and that what happened and happens to these innocent people could have happened to us or could happen to our families. As soon as I fall asleep, everything I imagine turns into a frightening nightmare, as if it were reality."

Rawya approached me and embraced my arms.

"Me too! Every story I hear, I dream about it and live it as if it were a reality and not a dream," I said

"When will this pain end?"

"I don't know if it will end one day or if it will accompany us for the rest of our lives."

***

Rawya and I were in constant contact with our families in Iraq. We also followed the news on television and social media. The good news started coming when we learned that Barack Obama gave the green light to the coalition forces to bomb ISIS positions and prevent them from advancing towards Kurdistan. The Kurdish Peshmerga also had a heroic role in defending valiantly for Kurdistan and obstructing the advance of the ISIS terrorist organization. As this aerial bombardment and resistance shown by the Kurdish fighters led to the retreat of the ISIS terrorists and forced them to retreat away from Duhok, where our families are displaced.

Lotta called me upon her returning from South Africa to check on me and my family. I told her that I was going back to work at Department of Chemistry tomorrow, but she asked me to rest for a few more days. I told her that I was tired of staying at home, and we agreed to meet the next day in the chemistry department.

***

Lund, Sweden, 26th of August 2014

In the morning, I went to the chemistry department. Lotta, Maggan and the rest of my colleagues were waiting for me in the corridor next to my office. I was very happy when I saw them, and I also saw joy in everyone's faces. Then Lotta chanted loudly with delight, "Hello, Firas!"

We hugged each other, and then Maggan and the rest of my colleagues hugged me. After that, I went to Lotta's office with Lotta and Maggan and had a cup of coffee. Both asked me to rest for a few days at home, if I wanted to. They also asked me to see a psychotherapist to help me get rid of the trauma that I was experiencing for fear that it would leave traces and negative impact on me in the future. But I didn't. This was a big mistake, as I became depressed. I started to speak less, whether at home or at work, and I had become more accustomed to isolation and sitting alone, with the thought that this life is trivial and not worth the trouble.

After I finished talking to Lotta and Maggan, I went to my office. My officemate, José, a postdoc from Spain, was sitting in the office. I entered the office and looked at my chair and the papers on the desk and scientific books paved on the shelves. I couldn't believe that I was here again.

I sat on the chair, put my hands on the desk, and then my mind was pulled somewhere else, to Iraq. It seems that I had been displaced by my mind for a long time, as I woke up to Jose patting on my shoulder with his hand. I turned to him and then he said to me in a calm voice, "It is okay, Firas! It's all over!"

On this day, I toured the corridors and laboratories of the Department of Chemistry, during which I met many colleagues and researchers, and we had brief conversations. I went to my bench to see that there were still many of my laboratory tools in place as I left them before I went to Iraq.

Then I went to the instruments that I had been working with. I checked the samples that I placed in refrigerators and freezers. I did all these things for the sake of my recovery and made a plan to start the work again. After a few hours, I felt that I no longer had the energy to continue and I ran out of energy, so I decided to go home.

***

Rawya and the kids were at home because the new school year had not started yet. Despite the wonderful summer atmosphere, we didn't have the energy, nor were we in a good enough mood to get out of the house. In the evening, when we were watching the news on TV, Enana was sitting on the floor playing in her toys, while Maxim was sitting on the sofa next to his mother and he was silently following the news. We were all quiet, except Enana, then suddenly Maxim said in a faint voice, "We must kill the bad guys."

Rawya and I were surprised. We both turned to Maxim, then I quietly asked him to repeat himself to make sure that I heard him correctly. "Dear Maxim! What did you say?"

"We must kill the bad guys," Maxim replied sharply this time.

We knew that by bad guys, he meant the Islamic State fighters, and we also knew that he was greatly affected by what happened, but we didn't realize that he had been impacted in such a negative way while he was still a little child.

"Me, you, my grandfather Antar, Fares, and Dilshad, must go and kill the bad guys," Maxim added.

"But we don't have the weapons to fight them," Rawya said as she tried to match him with the words and extract what was going on in his mind.

"Yes, we do! We have knives, which we can use to kill them," Maxim replied angrily, pointing to the kitchen where we keep the knives and looking at his fist, as if he was carrying a knife.

We were shocked when we heard Maxim's words. Enana stopped playing and looked at her brother, who was talking angrily. Rawya hugged Maxim as she tried to calm him down, while I got up and sat next to him. I tried to find the right words to make him stop thinking that negative way, but I failed. My own thoughts were riddled with violence and confusion. I thought the ISIS fighters deserved to be killed. If I had confrontation with them and had a weapon, I would not hesitate to kill them. But I didn't seek revenge as much as I sought justice. For me, justice at that moment meant that they all should be killed. As far as I was concerned, I knew that my thinking about committing murder was an abnormal one, and that if I had the opportunity to achieve justice, I would choose to do it through the law and not through my hands. Although achieving justice through the law is difficult and sometimes impossible.

It was unfortunate and sad that a young child had such an experience at this early stage of his life. I took the TV remote control and changed the channel that was broadcasting the news to another channel for children programs.

I looked at him and said, "Dear Maxim, we are safe now, as well as your grandmother Norra, grandmother Najah, grandfather Antar, and the rest of the family. They all are fine too. As for the bad guys, they will be defeated and get their fair punishment." I kept silent for few seconds and looked at him while I was smiling, then I added, "It has been a long time since you had your last training or played football. What would you think if we played football together tomorrow?"

"Okay!" Maxim answered.

Then, I looked at Enana, who was still staring at us, and then I heard the voice of Rawya chanting with joy, "What do you think of playing Uno now?"

Maxim and I chanted together, "Yes! Uno!"

Enana, who knew the game but didn't know how to play it, got up on the ground and chanted with joy, too, "Uno!"

Rawya brought the cards, and we all sat on the ground in a circle, and then Rawya started distributing the Uno.

***

That evening, after the children went to their beds to sleep, Rawya and I sat and talked about what Maxim said and decided that we would not listen to the news in their presence, and we would also avoid talking about what was happening in Iraq or even mentioning ISIS in front of the kids, especially in front of Maxim. And because we were still on summer vacation, we decided to go out for a picnic each day. In the following days, we went to Lomma Beach and Malmö Beach and we attended many musical activities organized by the municipality of Lund and the municipality of Malmö, in addition to the municipalities neighboring our city. We also went to the circus and played football. These daily excursions helped us somewhat restore our energy and prepare for a new phase, which we considered to be the post-ISIS stage.

I had a desire and motivation to go to work in the laboratory again. Rawya also went back to her studies. As for Maxim and Enana, the school year began, as well as their football training that we were keen to attend and watch the kids play.

***

Lund, Sweden, 9th of September 2014

On the 9th of September 2014, Lotta, Maggan and I organized a luncheon in the Department of Chemistry. Lotta sent an e-mail to all persons who participated in the rescue operation, as well as to my colleagues in the Green Technology Group and a number of friends. It was an invitation to a lunch banquet to thank everyone who contributed to our rescue and safe return to Sweden.

Rawya prepared food at home, where she excelled in preparing famous Iraqi traditional dishes such as dolma, biryani, kubba Mosul, Sheikh el-Mahshi, rice cooked in the Iraqi way, in addition to delicious and varied appetizers. The number of the invitees was more than twenty-five people.

Maxim and Enana were at school. As for me, I was helping Rawya to make appetizers, cut meat and vegetables, and get what she needed from the market. Maggan helped us to transport the food to Department of Chemistry, as our apartment was close to my work place. On that day, I prepared a presentation about the Yazidis and what was happening to them in Iraq.

Everyone attended, and we put the food on a long table. Everyone was looking at the delicious and varied dishes, smiling and asking about the names of these dishes. Rawya started giving an illustration of each dish and described its ingredients as a professional chef. Everyone was surprised when they knew that all these dishes were prepared by only Rawya.

Before starting the food, Lotta asked me, "Have you prepared the presentation regarding what happened in Iraq?"

"Yes! But I don't feel comfortable. Maybe I shouldn't do it," I answered with hesitation.

"Come on, Firas! Everyone here wants to know what happened," Lotta said and she encouraged me to give the presentation.

"Okay! But I think it is appropriate to give the presentation after lunch, otherwise this food will remain on the table and no one will have the appetite to eat."

"I agree with you! Okay! After the lunch!"

"Okay!"

Lotta turned to the guests and said with a smile, "The food looks delicious! Rawya has done a great job!"

"I hope you like it!" Rawya said.

"Should we start?" Lotta asked.

"Of course! please!" Rawya said.

Food was served as a buffet. The guests stood in a queue and started filling their plates and eating. They were asking Rawya about how to prepare each dish, including what ingredients and types of spices she used. About half an hour later, Lotta asked me to start the presentation. Most of the guests had finished eating while few other had not finished yet.

"Firas has prepared a presentation on what is happening in Iraq," Lotta announced.

I connected the computer to the projector, and then began displaying slides of the Yazidis' presence areas and other pictures showing what they were exposed to during the ISIS attack on their villages and cities, as well as while they were fleeing in Sinjar Mountain or displaced under bridges or in buildings under construction in Duhok and Erbil in Kurdistan.

The pictures were painful as everyone was affected, including some who cried, especially Rawya and Maggan. As for Lotta, tears poured out of her eyes and she could not help it, so she left the room to prepare coffee for everyone. Rawya also left the room loudly crying now. At the end of the presentation, I took the opportunity to thank Lotta, Maggan, Per, and everyone who helped me and my family to survive the ISIS terror. I found Rawya and Lotta hugging in the coffee room just outside, swaying from side to side. This was a difficult and heart-breaking moment for all of us.

This was the last time I talked about what happened. Several days ago, I did an interview with a Swedish radio station, but I didn't disclose my name because I was afraid, and when Per found out about this interview, he asked me and Lotta to not conduct any more interviews in future for security reasons, for the sake of my safety and that of my family as well. Therefore, Lotta and I decided to not speak to the press and to preserve the confidentiality of this rescue operation.

***

Lund, Sweden, Two years later, 5th of April 2016

It was two years filled with hard and diligent work, as I spent most of my time in the lab and my office to finish my studies on time. Rawya was also studying hard to finish her studies and obtain a Master's degree. The situation in Iraq hadn't changed. ISIS was still in control of Mosul, Anbar, and Salah al-Din, which represent almost a third of Iraq. The Peshmerga forces imposed their power and stopped the expansion of the Islamic State towards the Kurdistan region. As for my family and Rawya's family, they were constantly moving from one house to another in search of a place to settle, as they couldn't go back to their homes due to the cities still being under the control of the Islamic State.

On the 5th of April, it was three weeks and three days before I was to defend my thesis. This is the day when I will nail my thesis. The academic meaning of this is that the doctoral thesis, in its physical form, is made available to the public. This is a very old university tradition. With one copy of my thesis, a huge nail and a hammer, we all went to the outside of the library at the Chemical Center. Many colleagues from the whole department of chemistry were there, as well as some friends and my family. Abdulghani and Naseem were there, who also managed to finish their doctoral studies and obtain the PhD degree. The ceremony was led by Maggan and Lotta. I gave the hammer to Rawya to share with me this joyous moment in the nailing of the thesis, to thank her for her big role on this arduous journey. The hammer was also given to Maxim and Enana because they were an important reason for my happiness and provided a relief from the pressures of work during my studies.

***

Lund, Sweden, 29th of April 2016

On April 29th, 2016, I defended my thesis in lecture hall A in the chemical center. This is the same hall where Nobel Prize awardees in Chemistry every year come to give a lecture. My opponent was Professor Susan Olesik from The Ohio State University-USA, in addition to the examination committee, which was chaired by Professor Lo Gorton. After completing the thesis discussion that lasted for more than three hours, we headed to the lunch room in the Center for Analysis and Synthesis, where one of the administrators had prepared a table with drinks and snacks on it. Whereas the examination committee met in a room adjacent to the dining hall in order to make a decision to either accept or reject the thesis.

After waiting for nearly half an hour, the committee exited the room, and they were led by Professor Lo, who had a paper in his hand on which the final decision was written. At first, he stayed a little silent while staring at me. Everyone was silent, waiting to know the decision. I looked into his eyes and learned that he was trying to claim seriousness, but he could not control himself and laughed, then he said, "Congratulations! you passed!" We shook hands as everyone applauded, chanting with joy.

"Come on, please," Lotta said as she pointed with her hand to the table on which cognac glasses were placed. Then she asked everyone to lift their glasses to make a toast.

My colleagues gave me a gift that was wrapped. Lotta noticed that I was still tense and exhausted from the defending my dissertation, so she stepped towards me and said, laughing, "It looks like you need help!"

"Always!" I answered and laughed too.

Lotta helped me tear off the wrapping and when I opened the gift, I was surprised. The gift was a shirt for FC Barcelona – my favorite team. I liked the gift so much because it was the only shirt of the Barcelona team that has red and blue stripes horizontally and not vertically as usual. My name (Dr. FIRAS) was written on the back of the shirt as well as the number 16, referring to the year. My colleagues knew about my love for the Barcelona team, so I had a cup bearing the Barcelona logo, which was placed on the table in front of me when I was defending my dissertation, so they had planned to buy this gift a long time ago. I was so happy with this gift that even some of my colleagues said, "we felt you were happier to have this shirt than to get your doctorate."

***

Lotta's Story

Lund, Sweden, 29ᵗʰ of April 2016

It is a cold and humid afternoon, a typical April-weather in Sweden. I have just decided that I will wear a short party dress even though the temperature is not much over the freezing point, maybe five degrees Celsius. I am sitting in the kitchen in my house, thinking back on today's doctoral dissertation. I am so proud of Firas. He carried out such a nice discussion together with his opponent, Susan. Most PhD students I have supervised go through a process over several years of failures, learning, and struggles to publish articles. In the end, there is always a story to tell. I always try to tell that story during my speech in the evening during the PhD dissertation party. Now I am sitting here in the kitchen, summarizing Firas's story. This is quite a story to summarize. It goes beyond what is imaginable. Maggan and I have decided to give the speech together.

Kuria comes into the kitchen to ask me, "What are you doing? Why do you look so sad? We are soon going for the party!"

"Yes, I know. I am not sad, I am just thinking back on the whole rescue operation of Firas and his family. It is just so hard to believe that we actually managed to bring them home," I say with a melancholic voice.

"Okay, so what will you say in your speech?"

"I will just tell the story, together with Maggan. I hope that it will be good, and that Firas will not start crying. At least not too much," I say

"I remember when I once gave a speech to a previous PhD student I had in Uppsala. She cried so much during my speech that we had to take a break in the middle. I took her out to the bathroom asking her if I should just round off my speech. But she insisted that I continue. She liked it, but she got so emotional. It is a lot of pressure to write a thesis and defend it. When it is all done, it is like the tears just want to pour out," I say, almost talking to myself now.

"I know! I didn't cry during my party, but for sure I remember the stress." Kuria said.

"Yeah, I remember that you walked around outside in the middle of the night just before your dissertation. Sleeping problems, right?" I tell Kuria with a grin.

"Ha-ha, you are right, I almost forgot," he said.

We left by car, and Gabriel came with us. He brought his new iPad that made him so happy when he was allowed to use it. At the venue, there were already lots of people gathered, drinking wine. I spotted Firas and Rawya, and walked up to them to give them both a big hug. Rawya started crying a bit, and I wonder if she will always cry when she sees me.

"Welcome! Here you go," Firas says and gives me a glass with white wine.

"Thank you, Firas! How does it feel now? Are you relaxing now?" I ask him with a smile.

"Yeah, it feels good now! I am doctor now!" he tells me with smile on his face.

That is genuine happiness, I think to myself. Now we can really say: Mission Completed. Now Firas is a doctor in philosophy. No one could stop him. Not even ISIS.

***

"Cling, cling, cling," I try to get attention over the large crowd of dinner participants, which include colleagues, friends, Firas and his family.

"Good evening all of you! It is time for the supervisors' speech," I say with a loud and clear voice. Maggan is standing next to me, and we are facing Firas and Rawya.

"Firas did his Master degree project with us in 2011. His project was on blueberry... or was it bilberry? At least it is still visible in the ceiling of our high pressure fluid lab... but not until 2012 this project was done... at least almost..." I say reading from my notes that I had made earlier this afternoon.

Firas laughed a bit, maybe embarrassed about the never-ending bilberry project. No, he looks quite happy and curious about the continuation of the speech.

"Firas enrolled as a PhD student in October 2011, but in reality, he started in Lund in January 2012. And the bilberry project was still his project..." I continue talking, more relaxed now.

"Maggan and I received the first bilberry manuscript draft in March 2013, the second draft in May 2013, the third or fourth draft in November 2013. Then more experiments were needed... The year of 2014 started. Firas, as well as us supervisors, were all getting stressed about the never-ending bilberry story... Finally, the manuscript was submitted in February 2015 to the Journal of the American Oil Chemists' Society, and it was accepted as a research article in April 2015, exactly one year ago..." I explain with my most declamatory voice, and the whole crowd is laughing now.

I look up from my notes and decide to not look at them anymore. The rest of my speech will come directly from my heart.

"In July 2014, something happened that would turn out to have huge consequences for Firas and his family. Firas's wife, Rawya, went with the children to Iraq for a wedding. Firas was in the middle of stressful lab work with a Vitamin D project and the bilberry project. As you all probably know, ISIS advanced into the Sinjar region of Iraq and there was an extremely dangerous war situation," I explain with a much calmer and concerned voice now, trying to not become too emotional to be able to continue. I can see that Rawya is already sobbing, and Firas's eyes are filled with tears that will soon overflow and pour down, just like the rain that has started pouring down outside the windows.

I continue, "On the 6th of August, Firas manage to catch a flight to Iraq and he entered the Sinjar region. He wanted to save his wife and children. On the 8th of August, I received a SMS from Firas saying that 'if I'm not back in Sweden within three weeks, cancel my graduate studies.' So, the fact was that ISIS were in Duhok, and they performed a Yazidi genocide. They killed men and captured women and children. Firas's bank account was empty after helping the family to flee in Iraq."

All the guests are completely silent. I can see that Professor Lo is filming this speech. I can also see that some people are sobbing or crying. Rawya is crying a lot. I think about whether I should stop my speech now since so many people are crying. This is supposed to be a nice evening celebrating a PhD. I look at Maggan, and since we can communicate without talking because of working so close for several years now, we both agree to continue this emotional speech.

"When I received that SMS, I was thinking about just one thing: No way will ISIS prevent someone for getting a PhD! Science and the academia are an international sphere where religion and political standings should not matter," I say with a loud voice. This feels like the most important statement in the whole speech. Maybe the most important statement in my whole life. Plus, it is written in the Swedish

Higher Education Ordinance that all doctoral students have the right to defend their PhD thesis.

I continue, " On the 11th of August, I contacted administrators and bosses like Gunilla and Ola, who are both here tonight. Most importantly, I contacted Per, our security manager at Lund University. It turned out that Lund University has agreements with several security companies who can arrange transportation all over the world, even when there is a full-scale war. Within days, we had a contract with a transport company on the ground in Iraq."

"Firas had to answer a lot of security questions about how they were doing, if they had food and water, if they had their passports, if there were militaries around and what kind (Kurds, ISIS or what), and if the roads were blocked by military." I am talking completely free from my script now.

"Firas and I exchanged so many SMS during these few days. I also find out that I am an angel!" I say with a big smile, looking at Firas. "I had no idea that was the case!" I add with a grin.

"So finally, some days later, the transportation was arranged. Two SUVs with four armed men and bulletproof vests for the whole family entered Duhok to take the family to Erbil airport. And then, on the 19th of August, with a flight early in the morning from Erbil to Ankara, then to Istanbul, and finally to Copenhagen, the whole family traveled with anonymous flight tickets. They landed in the afternoon! As simple as that!" I say, almost looking like a wizard now.

If this had been four hundred years ago, now would be the moment that someone would start shouting "witch, she is a witch," and the whole crowd would grab me and set me on fire or something. I look at Maggan, and she knows that it is her time to speak.

Maggan talks about what happened next, from the arrival in Copenhagen airport, to the drive back to Lund and the safety check of Firas's family's apartment. She also talks about her relation to Firas and his research. I listen with one ear now. My eyes sweep over the crowd. I can see that everyone is listening with full attention. This speech is a bit long, I am thinking while I stand there next to Maggan. Professor Lo is still filming. I feel happy that he is here together with all of us. He is one of the famous professors of analytical chemistry, and it means a lot that he is sharing this moment with us.

All of a sudden, Maggan is looking at me, and her eyes are telling me that it is my time to round off this speech now. I have kept the most emotional part to the end. At least it is the most emotional part for me. I sense what I hold in my left hand. It is a small guardian angel in gilded brass. I look at Firas and Rawya, and I start to speak:

"There are angels. Yazidis believe in God and seven holy angels. Firas told me that I am an angel. At my father's funeral, I was given two guardian angels made in brass from the priest. One angel is for Firas to remember that there is always hope. There is always an angel out there for a person not feeling good, or a person having a difficult time. My own experience some years back is that I could not have a second child. At the same time, my father became very ill and he passed away on 12th of March 2007. On the 26th of December that same year, my second child was born, 259 days after my father died. An angel must have been involved. The name of our son is Gabriel, who is quite a famous angel in some religions," I say, trying to not start crying because of the emotions dwelling up inside of me. I look at Firas with my eyes full of tears.

"I give you this angel to always guard you and your family," I say to Firas. "I should also tell you how I cleaned this brass-made angel. I used tomato ketchup and rubbed it! The weak acids in tomatoes, like citric and ascorbic acid, removes tarnish and dirt from brass," I say with a grin while I give him the small shiny angel and a big hug. Firas looks at me, speechless with both joy and tears in his eyes, and he hugs me back.

This was quite a story to tell in a speech, I think to myself when the whole crowd is applauding. With lots of mixed emotions; sadness, happiness, and pride, I walk towards the dance floor. Ready to hit this party. Mission completed, for sure! The party can start!

***

Firas's Story

Lund, Sweden, 26ᵗʰ of April 2016

It was a wonderful and moving speech. I cried and Rawya cried, everyone cried as everyone was affected. After finishing the speech and we had dinner, the music was played, and everyone started dancing. There was a small stage in the hall. Rawya, Maggan, Lotta, Ola, Lo, and I went up to the stage to dance, while the guests were dancing in the ballroom. Rawya was wearing high-heeled shoes so she felt tired. She stepped towards me and said, "I am tired because of my shoes and I can't dance."

"Okay! Take them off!" I said.

Rawya took off her shoes and threw them aside. Ola, who was dancing with passion, looked at what Rawya did, and he liked the idea, thinking that Rawya wanted to dance barefoot. He took off his shoes too. Then Lotta and Maggan did the same. Everyone was dancing barefoot, except me. Ola looked at me and pointed with his hand that I should take my shoes off too. I took off my shoes, laughed, and kept on dancing. It was a special party that lasted until three in the morning.

***

2016 was a special year. I had achieved my dream of getting a PhD, despite all these difficulties and challenges that

I went through during my studies. In Iraq, the Peshmerga forces were able to defeat ISIS and free Sinjar, Bashiqa, Bahzani, and all the villages inhabited by the Yazidis. The Iraqi army and the Popular Mobilization Forces, PMF, also managed to liberate Mosul, Anbar, and Salah al-Din. ISIS had been expelled from Iraq and all lands under its control have been liberated. But the fate of more than 6,000 Yazidi women and children who were in the grip of ISIS remained unknown as ISIS fighters had moved them all to Syria, the last bastion of ISIS.

A year after my PhD graduation, I got a job at a pharmaceutical company in Malmö. Rawya finished her Master studies in biochemistry and got a job as researcher at Lund University. As for Maxim and Enana, they were still playing football in Lund football club, Lund FF. Maxim had developed significantly and had great football skills. His coaches liked him and admired him so much that one of his coaches named Johan told me that Maxim has a "warrior heart" and that he is confident that in the future he will sit in front of the TV and watch Maxim playing football.

***

The rescue mission took place in 2014 but, for security reasons, had only come to light in December 2018. Although I am no longer a student at Lund University, my relationship with my former supervisors, Lotta and Maggan, has not ceased, as we communicate from time to time. One weekday I got a message from Lotta:

> "Hello Firas! Are you okay? A journalist at the radio would like to talk to you regarding the rescue operation in 2014, who has been my friend for many years. Her Name is Hedvig Nilsson. She would like to make a documentary for the radio. Is it okay? Regards, Lotta."

> "Dear Lotta, I am fine! Thanks. I have got a new job as Analytical Scientist at pharmaceutical company in Malmö ☺. I hope you and your family are well. Regarding the journalist, yes, it is ok. Regards, Firas."

> "Congrats on your job! ☺I wonder if we can meet the journalist Hedvig the 27 or 28 February? Cheers, Lotta"

I had spoken to Rawya about this interview. I know that it is difficult for her to talk about what happened. Whenever she remembers what happened, she starts crying. I had even avoided talking about it for a long time. Rawya suggested that we do the interview in our house, especially since she missed seeing Lotta.

"You can do the interview here in our house. I miss Lotta. I'll prepare dinner for you all. I know that Lotta likes my food," Rawya said as she was excited.

"It is a good idea. Lotta suggested February 27 or 28 for the interview. Does this work for you?"

"Yes! Tell them to come at six in the evening and that dinner will be served at seven."

"Good!" Then I sent a message to Lotta, "Hi, Lotta! Thank you! Yes, we can. 27 or 28, both are ok! We will have a dinner at my place. Kind regards, Firas."

"Okay perfect! ☺"

Then a few minutes later I received another SMS from Lotta: "Hello again! Regarding the interview with Hedvig, we decided the 27th!"

"Okay! Regards, Firas"

***

At six in the evening, Rawya finished preparing dinner, while I prepared salads as usual. Maxim and Enana were watching TV when the doorbell rang. Hedvig and Lotta had arrived. Hedvig had the recorder in her hand, and as soon as she entered the house, she started recording all the conversations, even the side ones. After dinner, we sat in the living room. As for the children, they went straight to their room.

"How did you feel when you received the first SMS from Firas?" Hedvig asked Lotta.

"What was happening was completely unacceptable. I got so angry that ISIS was pushing itself into our world, exposing my doctoral student and his family to this, and disrupting the research," Lotta answered.

"What did you feel when you first saw two cars with armed men come to save you and your kids?" Hedvig asked Rawya.

"It was very hard to decide. Should I go to Sweden or I should stay here with my family? If something bad happened, then I wanted to be with them. If they die, then we will all die together," Rawya said and she was crying. Then she added, "It was very difficult decision, but I had to think about my kids."

Maxim and Enana were still sitting in their room, but they were listening to the interview. They were children, so it was usual for them to be curious and want to know what was going on around them. Hedvig asked if she could talk to kids. I went to their room and it was very obvious that they were standing behind the door and listening to us. I smiled and then asked them, "Hedvig wants to talk to you. Is it okay?"

"Okay!" Enana said while Maxim agreed by nodding his head.

During dinner, Hedvig and the kids had a chance to talk about many things such as school, football, music, and foods. The kids felt more comfortable talking to Hedvig. They went out from their room and sat next to Hedvig.

"Did you remember what happened in Iraq?" Hedvig asked Maxim.

"I will never forget that thing. Two big cars came and took us to another place. Then they took us again from that place to the airport. I was very afraid because I was thinking that something bad was going to happen, but it didn't happen. I remember it was very hot and there was war. We wanted to come to Sweden because there is no war here. And I remember my mom was always crying," Maxim answered.

"Do you see that your mother is sad when you talk about Iraq?"

"Yes!" Maxim said.

"She is a little happy here," Enana also said

"Do you understand the reason for her grief when you talk about Iraq? Hedvig asked both Maxim and Enana.

"I know. She does not want to be a war there. And because she came from there, she is missing her family and that's why I think she is sad," Maxim said

"I think she is sad because one day I saw her crying and when I asked her why, she said that she missed her mother and that she was unable to go there," Enana said.

Then Hedvig turned to me and asked, "What do you think about what people at Lund University did for you?"

"They are my heroes. They brought me back to Sweden and we are saved because of them. They really did something great. Something that I will never ever forget about it.

So, I hope that I can do great things in the future to make them proud of me."

"Do you want to say something to Lotta?"

"In 2014, my life was stopped and everything that happened after 2014 is because of Lotta. She really saved my life and my family as well. Not only that, but she also saved my future. She is my angel."

"Could you say the last sentence in Swedish?" Hedvig asked me.

I looked at Lotta and we both smiled. Then I said, *"Hon är min ängel!"*

The End

HISTRIA
BOOKS

Gaudium Publishing
Books to challenge and enlighten

THE
DOWNFALL
NIKLAS HAGEBACK
OF CHINA
OR CCP 3.0

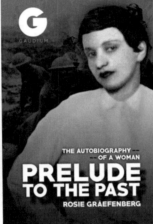

THE AUTOBIOGRAPHY
OF A WOMAN
PRELUDE TO THE PAST
ROSIE GRAEFENBERG

NIKLAS HAGEBACK
THE
DEATH DRIVE
Why Societies Self-Destruct

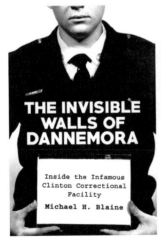

THE INVISIBLE WALLS OF DANNEMORA
Inside the Infamous Clinton Correctional Facility
Michael H. Blaine

ALL RISE!
THE LIBERTARIAN WAY WITH JUDGE JIM GRAY
JUDGE JAMES P. GRAY RET.
FOREWORD BY CONGRESSMAN TOM CAMPBELL

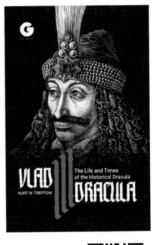

VLAD
KURT W. TREPTOW
The Life and Times of the Historical Dracula
DRACULA

FOR THESE AND OTHER GREAT BOOKS VISIT
HISTRIABOOKS.COM